Advance praise for *Lyrics of Lament*

"From the Bible to the blues, from the ancient Near East to modern New Orleans, from the Qur'an to Bob Dylan and Bruce Springsteen, Nancy Lee shows us the pervasive power of lament. The book is remarkable not only for its range but for its ability to marry eloquence with urgency, and clear thinking with impassioned prose."

Tod Linafelt
Georgetown University

"*Lyrics of Lament* puts into our hands compelling, musical speech for peace and hope. Nancy Lee uncovers exquisitely-honed poetic instruments to express grief, to struggle for faith, and to find God in the realities of deep suffering across the world. From Jeremiah to Lamentations to the Qur'an to African-American spirituals to rap, Lee calls forth language and form for the healing of the earth. This is a book for everyone."

Kathleen M. O'Connor
William Marcellus McPheeters Professor of Old Testament
Columbia Theological Seminary

"Like the kingdom scribe who brings out of the treasure what is old and what is new, Lee has gathered laments from as long ago and far away as Mesopotamia and biblical Israel, and as recently and close to home as New Orleans and New Jersey. This veritable treasury of human tears is poignant testimony to the enduring power and validity of the need to cry out to God in pain."

Rolf Jacobson
Associate Professor of Old Testament
Luther Seminary

Lyrics of Lament

From Tragedy to Transformation

Nancy C. Lee

Fortress Press
Minneapolis

LYRICS OF LAMENT
From Tragedy to Transformation

Scripture quotations are from the New Revised Standard Version Bible, copyright © 1989 by the Division of Christian Education of the National Council of the Churches of Christ in the USA. Used by permission. All rights reserved.

Quotations from the Qur'an are from *The Holy Qur'an*, transl. Abdullah Yusuf Ali, from the Online Quran Project <http://al-quran.info>.
Reprinted by permission of the Online Quran Project.

Cover image: © copyright iStockphoto.com/*Cry* by Craftvision
Cover design: Joe Vaughan
Book design: PerfecType, Nashville, Tenn.
For additional resources related to this title, visit fortresspress.com/lee.

Library of Congress Cataloging-in-Publication Data
Lee, Nancy C.
    Lyrics of lament : from tragedy to transformation / Nancy C. Lee.
        p. cm.
    Includes index.
    ISBN 978-0-8006-6301-8 (alk. paper)
    1. Laments—History and criticism. 2. Laments in the Bible. I. Title.
    BL560.L44 2010
    208—dc22
                                    2009044517

Manufactured in the U.S.A.

14 13 12 11 10 1 2 3 4 5 6 7 8 9 10

*This book is dedicated to the millions of people on Earth
whose extreme suffering is not seen and whose cries of lament are ignored,
whose voices cannot be raised for fear of imprisonment or death.
May each of us reach out to help these—our neighbors
whom we are to love—and change the systems of injustice.*

Contents

Foreword

Nancy Lee has committed her scholarly life, her open heart, and her alert mind to the voice of pain as it has sounded through the centuries and as it sounds now around our contemporary world of violence and exploitation. The beginning point for her work is the literature of lament in the Bible. But she moves easily and regularly out beyond the Bible to other ancient sacred literatures and to contemporary life and then back again to the Bible. She shows how the lament as an address to God is, at the same time, the most elemental and recurring human voice of dignity, self-affirmation, and hope. She attends to what is the most common and shared of all human voices. Her new book is an important resource for our own society which, for the most part, chooses denial rather than candid cry. Lee invites others in compelling ways to attend to the deep ache that characteristically permeates our life in the world.

I believe that scholarship is led—albeit at a slow pace—by the compelling questions that face faith and culture. Nancy Lee is among the foremost of a new generation of scholars who have paid primary attention to the laments in the book of Psalms. The reader of this volume may ponder why it is that Lee and her companions now bring so much sustained energy to this topic. There is remarkable ferment around these texts, of which there was scarcely a hint two decades ago. I have no doubt that the reason for that interest is that our culture—in the United States, in the U.S. church, and in Western culture more generally—is now witnessing a profound sense of loss, as old norms and categories of faith and meaning erode or are overwhelmed. The huge public issue of terrorism, the occasional outbreak of neighborhood violence that bespeaks unprocessed rage and anxiety, the peaceable diversification of culture, and the pervasive personal loss now so acute amid economic displacement all converge to make present U.S. culture a venue for loss for those who have been privileged in older social patterns. Lee has chronicled the emergence of lament in more violent societies. But the loss is acute here as well, even if not as palpable or as dramatic. Such loss must, perforce, be grieved. And these old poem-prayers still provide the best script for such grieving that must of necessity be vocal and public.

Lyrics of Lament is a fine example of an intense scholarly project, but at the same time it addresses a need that is broadly felt among us. Of course there are those who do not experience the present collapse of old norms and categories as loss, but as emancipation. Lament is not for them. But there are more than enough people who face this loss so as to warrant not only this book but the eruption of new scholarship that is all around it as well.

As Lee recognizes, the laments in the Bible are faith-specific to the God of Israel. That specificity, however, is both located in and generative of a much broader practice. It is located in a broader practice in that it draws upon the long-standing custom of ancient Near Eastern lore; this much has been recognized for generations. But the faith specificity of biblical lament is also, as Lee shows so well, generative of a much broader stream of giving voice, in that the biblical laments have evoked other, more contemporary laments. As a result, the specificity of synagogue and church remain expressive of and deeply connected to a larger human practice of crying out. This connection makes possible a case study in the continuing question of the particular and the universal. Laments must of necessity be specific to pain and loss, and Israel's laments are specific to the displacement of exile and the continuing alienation of the Jews. But they are universal in that every society knows about loss, displacement, and alienation. In this study, the human cry is shown to be connected to the insistent tone of a Jewish cry. The sense of loss is universal; the way of utterance is particular. Lee's great gift to us is to have focused on this connection and led us into its richness. The outcome is a study deeply rooted but immediately practical in a society that is tempted to numbness, silence, and denial. Lee shows how honest practices of grief are the way to newness. The voiced, public grief of the lament is a prerequisite for beginning again in hope.

Walter Brueggemann

INTRODUCTION

Song for Sudan

Anonymous

. . . the planes dropped the bombs before daybreak—
the janjaweed stormed
with the dawn.
those who could
fled to the forest
to hide till they'd gone.
returning to ruins by moonlight
she found she was orphaned and then—
there they began their exodus out of sudan . . .
she watched herself widowed while guarding their sleeping
    children—
. . . magboula rocks under the tree
no food for the child she cradles—staring at me.
what will it take to remember—what we said we'd never forget.
never again, is now,
once again in sudan . . . [1]

The inheritance

Kisan Sosa, India

The stale old air we have inherited
The helpless prayer, we have inherited.

As a ceiling we got rusted tin
The wall of fear, we have inherited.

The back got the dried river of sweat
And the eyes had inherited the empty well.

The thirst in the corridor and in the house hunger
The mind had inherited the desire for a silent cry.

Where the self-esteem is wounded and screams,
Lying in a bleeding corner, we have inherited.

Wherein so many snakes move and move
that black box, we have inherited.

Come on, let us turn into a sun and set afire
The night that is a nightmare, we have inherited. [2]

Back Water Blues

Bessie Smith, New Orleans

When it rained five days and the skies turned dark as night
. . . There was trouble takin' place in the lowland at night
I woke up this mornin', couldn't even get out of my door. . . .
Enough trouble to make a poor woman wonder where she's gonna go
They rowed a little boat . . . about five miles across the farm . . .
I packed up all of my clothes, throwed them in, and they rowed
    me along
Where it thundered and . . . the wind began to blow . . .
There was thousands of people,
They had no place to go. . . .
I looked down on the house where I used to live.
Back Water Blues that calls me to pack my things and go
. . . There ain't no place for a poor woman to go. [3]

Two songs and a poem convey but a trace of suffering in today's Sudan, India, and New Orleans. The first two are translated into English; the second gives a not very widely-heard Dalit perspective (the so-called "untouchables"). These lyrics of lament tell the stories of people's suffering through the voices of poets and singers. Usually neglected, the graphic descriptions in these lyrics of distress want the world to know, appealing to human hearts for help. Most at risk are the children, women, the sick, the poor, and the elderly. Men suffer too.

People had prayed laments for millennia in ancient cultures prior to the Abrahamic religions. Yet, the Hebrew biblical tradition of ancient Israel produced a living treasury of lament prayers and liberation-justice traditions. These have been passed down to significantly shape the early form and theology of lament prayer in monotheistic Christianity and Islam, as well as subsequent Jewish laments during long periods of their persecution throughout history. The ancient Israelite lament tradition would be adopted by communities oppressed in Africa, the Americas, and Asia. Sorely acquainted with oppression by white slave-traders, owners, and the dominant discriminatory culture, these communities could build on the Hebrew model to innovate new forms of lament that would shape music and fund liberation movements in cultures worldwide. In Islam, the flowering of prayer five times per day was instituted, including development of the *du'ā'*, or lament-type prayer of supplication.

At its core, the biblical lament model is one of appealing to God for help, for sustenance, rescue, and inspiration, especially in the face of suffering and injustice. Yet even this bedrock is not without its fault lines to which our lives today might make needed adjustments—especially with regard to the troubling elements of vengeance and violence in some texts, implicitly or explicitly joined to God's purpose. This book will attend to these matters, both in their illumination of the human psyche and their dangerous position on the edge of a deep chasm of darkness. Yet, no spiritual heritage or sacred text is without its troubling elements, or limited human perspective, or without its cultural share of wrongdoing—whether Jewish, Christian, Muslim, or any other tradition. This book is, therefore, unlikely to appeal to the purists or the literalists. Nor is it for those who think they are right while everyone else is wrong, or that they are "more right" than others. The sacred texts that crystallized God's inspired word through prophets or other voices might gravely criticize then-current practices or peoples. It is surely time to admit that a universal condemnation of a whole culture, religion, or people, along with a supersessionism by its own group claiming God's favor, is a limited human perspective with deadly consequences, but is not God's perspective. More often, it is a political tool to maintain power. Perhaps it is an insult even to God to say there is only one true religion, or a "truest" religion; better, there are "true relationships" with God. We are all in this together, as the interrelationships on the living earth show, in our suffering, in our wrongs, and in our resilient and faithful contributions. And often enough, it is the nonreligious who make great contributions in support of humanity and creation.

At this writing, the world has heard the heartbreaking lament of a Palestinian doctor in Gaza who lost his daughters to a bombing, just as he went on the air live with his regularly scheduled interview on Israeli television. Unceremoniously observed on cable television worldwide and on YouTube, that awful and unspeakable moment—with his broken, frantic cry of lament in Arabic and Hebrew asking repeatedly, "O God, what have we done to them!?"—has sent many human beings into a deep examination of conscience and sorrow about what we value, after all. What are we all willing to protect for each other, our neighbors in the human family? It brings out again the many grievances suffered by all sides in such situations. That moment could just as easily have been the coverage of a bomb landing in Israel to devastating effect, or American bombs devastating homes and families in Iraq, or a tragic scene of death in the aftermath of the September 11 attack on the World Trade Center in New York. In the contexts of lament considered here, decades after the "Never Again" of the Holocaust, vast numbers of world citizens, and an alarmingly increasing number, have suffered or died due to failed political leadership. The screams of millions of people of Rwanda went unheard. Today, the Sudan groans to be rescued from the throes of genocide, while some perpetrators of genocide from Rwanda contribute to atrocities in the war in the Democratic Republic of the Congo, where millions have already died.

And what of Iraq and Afghanistan, and their years of misery? Where are the voices of people suffering from war, yet who are not responsible for causing it? What of the suffering of everyday Palestinians and Israelis? There is mostly a vast silence imposed, punctuated by distracting noises of the media, the military, the politicians' sound bites, and the ongoing explosions of violence by extremists. While the voices of the people surely cry out, they are virtually unheard in the international community beyond their countries.

This book will show how human beings throughout history and across cultures and faith traditions have forged channels and rituals for lament into a rushing river that cannot be held back. They have created compelling, beautiful, and sublime expressions of sorrow and protest. Using genres and lyrics of lament, they have processed painful tragedy, and in so doing have found the hope to join together in transforming society with calls for change and justice, appealing for human and divine intervention through the power of music, prayer, and song. This book will build on, yet move beyond, academic and expert preoccupations, to share the people's authentic voices of lament. The great irony is that millions of people around the globe simply long for the same things in life. It is time for the people's will to outweigh the politicians and their systems of power.

A few preliminary words are in order. No single book on lament from around the world can be comprehensive, and yet this is an attempt, as perhaps never before, to bring the varied laments of the human family under one canopy. (Readers will have their own suggestions of laments to add for greater representation, and these are welcomed.) Only the expanse of sky can contain them all, and believers might say that only Allah/God/Adonai/the Great Spirit hears them all. Those lamenting sometimes surely wonder if they are heard. Not all, but very many of the poems and songs here have been translated into English from their native languages. English is not necessarily preferred; it is only pragmatic for bringing together a larger participating audience. As the axiom goes, poetry cannot be translated. And so we rely on the gifts of trusted translators, as well as the poets and lyricists themselves, to approach and suggest meanings. Meanings continue to be constructed in the ongoing transcendent interplay between words and rhythm and music, and the hearer's interpretation, perhaps inspired anew by the Spirit or the Muse.

Regarding this author's background, as well as my views toward the cultures, religions, and spiritual ways of life whose multiple voices of lament are herein given, one cannot help but struggle with a presumptuousness of claiming to understand an expression that is not from one's own tradition. As far as possible, I wish the voices to speak for themselves, with some added information about genres and context, and shared features and differences across cultures and religions. The primary motivating factor for this work is that so many countless voices of suffering in our world are largely neglected or unheard. Any errors are mine alone, and where this occurs, I ask for pardon, as I sought to find common ground while still respecting important differences.

I believe we humans stand to benefit today from the experiential wisdom of the many peoples and cultures which came before us and that surround us, while each of us may also devoutly claim a specific heritage. Mine is Christian, yet my calling is to work in the field of Hebrew Bible and in religious studies in relation to cultures, society, and justice issues. I am an American and am sometimes ashamed when our failures of humility and action—individual, political, and religious—do not live up to sacred principles. I have lived elsewhere and seen a fair amount of the world, often spending time in appalling living conditions. Indeed, it is just in such places (found in every country, of course) where I have seen the most inspiring, resilient, faithful, and hopeful people—whether in Bosnia-Herzegovina, with its beautiful mix of Muslims, Jews, and diverse Christians finding healing after war and a recent terrible genocide, or in South Africa, with its extraordinary victory for a people so long oppressed yet forming a rainbow nation, or among Native Americans who remain true to a sacred wisdom that we all need. I am inspired by Gandhi's vision that we are all children of God and can learn from one another. With H. Richard Niebuhr, I believe that though we abide in and grow from the roots of the internal history we claim, both criticizing and contributing to it, we must envision and practice a humility that recognizes that no one has the complete truth of God (this would be idolatry); we need one another in order to make the fullest understanding, and life, possible. Such "radical monotheism" is not to diminish the truths of Christianity that I or others hold, nor is it to find no truth in those who practice spiritual traditions that diverge from "monotheistic" language or understandings. I have found that people in their late teens and twenties are as eager for a broader, respectful approach as many of us older ones are.

The book gives many examples of lament in poems and songs and sacred texts (see also the endnotes for each chapter), and the book's companion website (www.fortresspress.com/lee) contains links to many of these so the reader may view or listen to a performance, or so a teacher may create a relevant syllabis. I owe a debt of gratitude to a great many artists for allowing me to quote their lyrics and post their web links. (I have purposefully chosen to include laments from those whose work is an expression of the situation of suffering in which they have lived or are living.) Some of the web links are "hot," so that one click gives direct listening, either through an artist's web page or to YouTube; others will require the reader's choice of purchasing a single digital song at slight cost from a licensing company for personal use (for example, an MP3 through Amazon), or of subscribing for a monthly fee to a company's web site, thereby having ready access to full-length playing of many songs, such as through Rhapsody, Napster, and others.

Anthropologist Ruth Finnegan noted that three traditional types of songs are considered to be universal—in other words, that people across the globe sing them—the lullaby, the wedding song, and the lament (as in a dirge for the dead). In modern societies, especially in the West, lament lyrics are often considered "secular" if they do not refer to a divine realm or belief, or are not offered as prayer. Yet the line between secular and sacred is not always so easily drawn, as sometimes even a sacred lament is a sheer description of distress. Popular musicians or literary poets may lament with descriptions of suffering that reference prayers or pleas to the divine for help. The laments below are examples. The first, by the late Jewish poet A.M. Klein, is an excerpt from a lament about the unspeakable losses of the Shoah; the second is a lament describing loss of home by Iraqi poet Moayed al-Rawi; and the third is an excerpt from a lament prayer by the late Lakota holy man Black Elk.

Elegy

A.M. Klein

. . .

A world is emptied.
Marked is that world's map
The forest colour.
There where Thy people praised
In angular ecstasy Thy name, Thy Torah
Is less than a whisper of its thunderclap.
Thy synagogues, rubble . . . academies,
Bright once with talmud brow and musical
With song alternative in exegesis,
Are silent, dark. They are laid waste,
Thy cities, Once festive with thy fruit-full calendar,
And where Thy curled and caftan'd congregations
Danced to the first days and the second star,
Or made the marketplaces loud and green
To welcome the Sabbath Queen;
Or through the nights sat sweet polemical
With Rav and Shmuail (also of the slain)—
Oh, there where dwelt the thirty-six—world's pillars!—
And tenfold Egypt's generation, there
Is nothing, nothing . . . only the million echoes
Calling Thy name still trembling on the air.[4]

The Illusion of Place

Moayed al-Rawi

The home we used to live in had become a cave
smells like garlic
covered with lime and dirt
The wind that enters our home is humid
sticks to the body
and the water is putrid, stinks, full of poisonous bubbles.
That's what you said to me
But my home is not the place
Where the grouse can take refuge
there not only she dies but the soul too.
Thus we were expelled from our homes,
from the house that glowed with life,
dominated by mothers' love
We were driven by the rivers
to their deep streams

We return to where we started, to the rock
when the river lost control of its course
to be crucified next to the spring.
We see the wind choked inside the well
unable to find the shadow of a tree at noon
seeking protection from heat
We had become pawns, manipulated by Satan
driving us to suffering,
filling our hands with burning sands in hot summer.
We are the angels
deprived of light
repressed,
damned.
Our faces have wounds,
injuries of old time
showing the painful tattoos of many places
we were forced to leave
once and for ever.[5]

Earth Prayer

Black Elk, Lakota holy man

Grandfather, Great Spirit, once more behold me on earth and
　　lean to hear my feeble voice. You lived first, and you are
　　older than all need, older than all prayer. All things belong to
　　you—the two-legged, the four-legged, the wings of the air,
　　and all green things that live.

You have set the powers of the four quarters of the earth to cross
　　each other. You have made me cross the good road and road
　　of difficulties, and where they cross,
the place is holy. Day in, day out, forevermore, you are the life of
　　things.

Hey! Lean to hear my feeble voice.
At the center of the sacred hoop
You have said that I should make the tree to bloom.

With tears running, O Great Spirit, my Grandfather,
With running eyes I must say
The tree has never bloomed

Here I stand, and the tree is withered.
Again, I recall the great vision you gave me.

It may be that some little root of the sacred tree still lives.
Nourish it then
That it may leaf
And bloom
And fill with singing birds!

Hear me, that the people may once again
Find the good road
And the shielding tree.[6]

———— ✾ ————

"Hey, Lean to Hear My Feeble Voice" (Black Elk, page 86) from *Earth Prayers* by Elizabeth Roberts. Copyright © 1991 by Elizabeth Roberts and Elias Amidon. Reprinted by
permission of Harper Collins Publishers.

In general, not all prayer is "lament," but prayer as lament is practiced by holy leaders of traditional cultures, both in ritual format and in individual freer forms. Poets and popular singers are free to craft lyrics as they wish, but some orderly religious rituals—worship, mass, Shabbat, or prayer, especially in hierarchically determined religions or cultures—do not always give a place to the people's publicly performed lament with free improvisation. The powerful exceptions in cultures retaining traditional processes include the improvised "call and response" of many African and African-American churches, as well as the individual virtuosity of Muslim singers or imams leading prayer, and the people's sung responses. Yet rigid forms of religious ritual that restrict such speech will give way, collapse, in times of tragedy and catastrophe, as the spontaneous creation of lyrics of lament anguish forth. Virtually all traditional cultures have forms and rituals for regular lament (as prayer or as dirges for the dead). In modern western cultures, religious and secular realms are pushed apart from each other, and Christian communities often no longer sing laments for the dead and do not regularly sing lament prayers or songs (this is much less the case in so-called developing countries). Nevertheless, it is ironic that it is the popular song writers and poets, often more powerfully than the crafters of religious liturgies, it might be argued, who have been most responsive and flexible to adapt and compose new songs to meet the emotional and spiritual needs of sorrowing people. The song cited above, "Backwater Blues"—sung recently by the beloved New Orleans blues singer Irma Thomas, for the hurricane victims of Katrina in 2005—was actually composed and performed a long time ago by the great blues singer Bessie Smith. While it may have described any devastating flood, it came to be used to lament the devastating Mississippi flood of 1927. Now, it speaks anew to the hearts of those who suffered in New Orleans.

As numbed shock wears off after terrible tragedies, religious rituals appear less than adequate, at least in western cultures, to convey or process the immensity of lasting pain and loss. This is, to an extent, as it should be: words cannot express immense trauma, and silence somehow intones awe and respect for the mourners and the dead. It is said that Elie Wiesel could not write of his traumatic experiences of the Holocaust for ten years. In a recent interview, he suggested that silence, in response to great tragedy, may be the most appropriate response. In recounting the silences of Abraham, Aaron, and Job after the agonizing deaths or near deaths of their children in the Bible, Wiesel notes of Aaron, "What could he say? What can be said? . . . It is a kind of advice to us: In certain situations, silence is best." And yet, after silence, there comes utterance, questions, and lament. Wiesel says, "Silence is always breaking up. When you finally speak, when you open up, you break."[7] And then there was the unbearable silence from the bystanders, which allowed unspeakable devastations, as well as the silence of God. As we will see, in most traditions and cultures, these silences have also been the subject of lament.

In regular Jewish mourning rituals, a period of silence is respected and observed. Mourners are not expected to study celebratory parts of the Bible; they are limited to mournful passages such as Job, Lamentations, and parts of Jeremiah. Confessional lament prayers which suggest that mourners may have sinned are omitted as inappropriate. Such compassionate wisdom implies that to do otherwise, to proceed as usual or to expect participation in joyful praise music, for example, might violate the integrity of the mourner's sorrowful state, pouring salt into a delicate wound. Silence helps to curtail painful clichés. Instead, this tradition has been careful in its customs for processing grief. Care for such wounds includes silence, support, songs of sorrow, and prayers to God for help and comfort.

While there are some gifted leaders or performers who, in the aftermath of great social tragedy, sing and compose new songs for performance, the usual modus operandi by religious leaders in western, Christian cultures is to turn passively to the same musical repertoire they've always known. This is natural, for there is comfort in the familiar. But reaching only for "Amazing Grace" to salve immense sorrow (about a guilty ex-slave owner transformed by God)—and just a few standard, though beloved, hymns sung only in the fleeting moment of a funeral—is not enough for many people. There is a risk of diminishing a song's meaning to virtual cliché through its overuse. Poignant comfort is not just in the familiar, or reliance on some "static familiar," but in the "familiar made new," the familiar song made new both by added meanings of current sad circumstances, and the freedom of the human spirit to shape the familiar for one's new needs, infused by divine inspiration.

What could account for this tremendous absence of creative, lyrical expression for those who are suffering in so many western, especially Caucasian, communities and congregations of faith? Perhaps a life of comfort creates passive acceptance. This is especially surprising in America, which cultivated individual freedom and jazz. In Christian circles, one of the best examples of the ability to compose afresh or to renew lyrics while respecting familiar hymn tunes is Brian Wren's lyrics composed through the years.[8]

But perhaps the most impressive Christian example of fresh music that affirms lament is found in the black church traditions. Long ago, these traditions discovered the passionate practice of singing one's own song of suffering to God, drawing on biblical models, and using African call-and-response patterns, with freedom of improvisation, to express pain transformed into joy through spirituals and gospel praise songs.[9] For example, in South African black churches, the mere mention of a need or tragedy is enough to spontaneously start a song in response. And traditional cultures around the world, whether in Asia, Africa, or the Americas, often exhibit a genuinely vibrant faith and worship that is linked to a living oral traditional, popular process. There is something vital to be learned from practices that integrate the balance of lament and praise from the Judaic traditions of the psalms and biblical liberation narrative. Yet, more and more white Christian congregations are noticing the phenomenon of too much praise music in their repertoire to the virtual neglect of lament. In how many congregations can the walking wounded who need consolation really count on a sorrowful song at a certain point in every service? Or do dominant praise and hymns override all worship, thus preventing congregations from honestly facing the hardships that people are really dealing with in their lives?

A few anecdotes of experience will illustrate. On one occasion when I myself was struggling with a personal matter, I decided to attend a regular chapel service at the seminary where I was enrolled at the time. Upon seeing the bulletin that included a song called

"Lamentation," I sorely welcomed the promise that there would be some solace offered through this worship service. When that moment arrived, my hope was dashed when the singer performed a popular evangelical-type song built entirely on a single verse in the book of Lamentations that praises God and says all is fine. Nothing of the sorrow contained in the countless laments of that book of five chapters was expressed, and I left with despair added to my grief. The Christian liturgist did not understand the Hebraic lament tradition, or the need for parishioners to lament.

In 1996, I was living in Croatia and traveling throughout much of Bosnia on a Fulbright fellowship during the year just after the wars ended. People were struggling with the traumas of the devastation of war. I commonly encountered examples of extraordinary faith and courage in the face of unspeakable hardship and horrors. A young man, who was a music minister at a Protestant church, confided to me one day that, at the time of the military draft, he had served in the army to defend his country during the war. His experience of the violence was devastating, and he was very troubled. The problem of war veterans falling into alcoholism due to their unprocessed trauma and grief was common. In that traditional eastern European culture, therapy was still seen as somewhat taboo. The young man thought he might turn to his church and his pastor as a place where, through his music ministry, or song at least, he might find some solace for his own healing and also find a way to help others. When he suggested some sorrowful songs to the pastor, he was quickly dismissed and told that the church must emphasize positive music and the praise of God. At this rebuke, the young man fell into an unresolved despair laid on top of his inner, unprocessed trauma and suffering, and he painfully realized that his church's music was largely irrelevant for helping others who were as psychologically wounded as he was.

Yet, I am convinced that religious leaders across faiths are eager for their prayer or worship rituals to reflect the fullness of what people go through, including pain and sorrow, and of God's powerfully-felt grace. Some people may longingly hope that the static structures of prayer or of worship expectations simply handed on by rote repetition—those that may bind or box in the human spirit—will be broken through, exploded by a living, Spirit-driven experience that fires time-honored traditions with unfolding innovation. There is no doubt that such worship of God has been practiced at different times and places through the ages. Such music and prayer will tap the power of God's Spirit and propel people out into their communities and the world with a passion to alleviate suffering, and thereby embody welcome news for those in despair.

I am convinced that a turning point for a new era among communities of faith and our societies is to go beyond the simple but necessary reaffirmation of the *idea* of lament. It lies not only in recovery of the reading of lament texts and homilies and of praying lament. These are important; but a vital key—a linchpin—is in our lyrics, in our song, for as we know, it is music that powerfully transports the deepest longings of our hearts and souls into the presence and power of God, and drives our rebuilding of society and community. Yet again, music or singing in spiritual communities and in popular culture is, of course, commonplace, so neither is song alone the answer to transforming ritual and society.

The most vital link, in my view, is the *process of creating* laments—a process of restoring or returning to an empowerment of community members toward greater participation through the imperative of finding and expressing one's own lament song or poetry lyrics. Each must find his or her individual voice that expresses that suffering and brings him or her, with risk, into the heart of the community. This is faith; this particularly taps God's energy and power and makes for passionate and life-changing expression in the community. But frankly, religious communities must give individuals an outlet for this; religious leaders in positions of power who are gatekeepers of what is allowed for public expression or performance in ritual or liturgy might open the doors. Social communities do encourage and cultivate the creation of poetry and lyrics in safe gatherings. No matter what a community sings or prays, individuals can contribute and be transformed through a renewed, living oral traditional process. Otherwise, it will be easier to hide vulnerable selves in group-songs only, composed long ago, only rarely with fresh adaptation. In essence this may fail to encourage individuals to give themselves over and up to God, who waits to hear each and every voice, and to intervene, heal, and give new life.

"Teach to your daughters a dirge, and each to her neighbor a lament," God implored the women of Judah and the prophet Jeremiah at a most desperate hour. As these words suggest, divine wisdom—and even tough divine expectation—knows that human lament is necessary. Voicing loss and sorrow also may help curtail future violence, injustice, and human and social disintegration. Singing our sorrow and lament is necessary for our own faith and our diverse faiths, and ironically, for all of our efforts at serving and healing the world.

Chapter 1 considers the general universal practices of lament in ancient cultures, as well as in traditional cultures still existing around the world, and in some contemporary modern cultures. The chapter examines the two primary genres of lament—dirge, and lament prayer—and the important role of women in composition and performance; this chapter illuminates how oral traditional composing and performing works.

Chapter 2 explores a number of traditional features of both dirge and lament prayer genres that are shared across cultures and throughout history, and across religions, with many illustrations.

Chapter 3 examines the many ways in which lament is so central in the Hebrew Bible, and how it appears in the sacred texts of the New Testament and the Qur'an. Links of lament to the importance of justice in all three traditions are illuminated, with some examples of lament songs that have driven social justice movements in contemporary cultures.

Chapter 4 explores how lament shapes the biblical Psalms and prayer there, examines lament prayer in the New Testament and Qur'an, as well as contemporary lament prayer from diverse cultures.

Chapter 5 suggests how the prophets used lament, related to social justice.

Chapter 6 considers the ancient biblical book of Lamentations and gives historic and contemporary examples of peoples lamenting across cultures.

Chapter 7 addresses the problems of violence and revenge that can be latent in lament, both in sacred texts and in cultural expressions. Instead there is a call for the people of all cultures and faiths to innovate the genre away from any destructive tendency—while still maintaining its raw force—by composing for our time expressions of mourning seeking *nonviolent* justice.

Chapter 8 closes the book by giving inspiring examples of poets and singers of lament who are envisioning a world transformed from tragedy to unity and peace.

In the end, this book will press forward in challenging all people to lament, not just for ourselves and our own, but for all voiceless sufferers whose cries are not heard, thereby together working to make change for the common good.

This volume is indebted to the untiring work of poets, songwriters, performers, and translators; to anthropologists who illuminate and support the practice of lament across cultures worldwide; to those in religious studies who honor lament traditions in a range of situations; and to scholars in biblical and ancient Near Eastern studies, theology, liturgy, and therapy. I am indebted to my teachers in this area: Walter Brueggemann, Mishael Caspi, and many colleagues in the Society of Biblical Literature's "Lamentations in Ancient and Contemporary Contexts" group. I am especially indebted to my mentor and friend, the late Dr. Thomas W. Downing, Jr., who so eloquently addressed human suffering, toward dignity, resilience, and wholeness.

My thanks to my professor colleagues, Judy Grimes and Oliver Lawrence who have been supportive of a vision of the power of music and poetry to bring social justice and unity, and also to my students who have especially engaged these issues—Kyle Tade, Rachel Nelson, Soofia Ahmed, and Sean Proctor, and so many students who show keen interest in this topic. Great thanks to Neil Elliott, Joshua Messner, and Julie O'Brien at Fortress Press for their encouragement and support in getting this complex book produced.

Let us close this Introduction with a vocal and instrumental blues lament by Charlie Miller, the great trumpet player from New Orleans:

Prayer for New Orleans

Charlie Miller

Trumpet
Just a prayer for New Orleans,
Just a prayer for New Orleans.
Oh how I care for New Orleans,
yeah, yeah, yeah, for New Orleans.
Just a prayer for New Orleans,
Just a prayer for New Orleans.

If you see me, don't ya stare;
I'm from New Orleans.
Please don't stare, I'm from New Orleans.
Just a prayer for New Orleans,
Just a prayer for New Orleans. . . .[10]

PART ONE

Lament: Ancient and Contemporary Voices

CHAPTER ONE

From Dust to Dust—Common Ground: Suffering Is Universal

A Plea from Pain

Nancy C. Lee

Oh the woe . . .
How dare—why—one
raise the dead
open wounds
side by side?

. . . it is for you, man . . .
and you
and them and me
and all this human sea
each one . . . alone, bereft
threadbare, in despair,
adrift . . . on a rickety raft,
no accent's familiar sound,
no soul, no religion, to sell
just silent wind and sky

and wind-seared eye, dry, burning
. . . unable to see . . . over the swells
of tears, the expanse of sea . . .
languishing . . . for life
a drop of rain, a morsel of bread—
pining for Land
claiming God, in order to blame, superseding
all/each grappling, blessed and sinking,
into the deep,
come hell or high water—
Take it to heaven then—the strife,
drown every dreamed homestead,
with blood's vengeance and *right*,
so all Eden's cheap.

And yet . . . the dark Sea is immense
down there, with fiercer jaws,
when all is said and done,
better our extremities exposed
up here, in the quiet blue expanse . . .
though no rescue or escape. . . .

But there! gaunt Sorrow sits . . .
on the raft's other side,
under, the water laps (it's
no shame or honor to bear,
not here, no one sees or cares).
There's nothing, but haunting
memories . . . pain . . .
swollen grief from long ago
that no one should bear
from the deep it wells
. . . and wells
. . . lie down, weep and weep. . . .

Let me . . . languish and die . . .
I'm expended, so weak, no hope
no burial no lament no joy fulfilled.

Just then Sorrow shifts—
reaches for you, and lifts
you up
—look there! above the swells—
there's another—joy, you are saved!
there . . .
reach for your neighbor
who lives, if you can—
need the other, reach,
and—for my children.
We've been waiting so long—
God-given.
When you reach Land, *listen*—
lift them from the ground
of death and despair,
little bodies
soldiers
daughters
crumpled there,
love them all,
if you dare, if you deign:
my daughters . . . and Abel . . . and Cain.

—Eve[1]

Singers Lament Cities in Ruin on the Tigris and Euphrates

How ironic, in an age of technological sophistication never before seen across human culture, that our millions of words—daily surging through the Internet, via satellite, over the airwaves, saved on digital files, discs, and flash drives—may not stand the test of time, but may disintegrate. How ironic that ancient Sumerian cuneiform texts of lament, engraved on clay tablets and placed in safekeeping, have weathered all the millennia, even though some tablets have likely perished from foolhardy smart bombs and wartime looting.

Ironic and more vastly tragic is how, in spite of human technology, for all its supposed "democratizing" impact, the specific laments of the millions of people suffering where the spotlight has long shone *cannot be heard*, indeed, in this "cradle of civilization." With an absence of heard dirges and laments, a dearth, really, coinciding with a looming demise of traditional cultures around the world, there is virtual silence. Is there so little compassion that technology is not made to serve humanity rather than destroy it?

So common is human suffering around the globe that where one lament goes unheard or disappears, seven more are sure to take its place. No doubt, the powers that be across the nations in government, military, and media know that airing the voices of lament is dangerous and may unleash demands for change, or calls for an end to power always having its way at the expense of the powerless and often innocent masses, subjected to endless cycles of war, oppression, poverty, and suffering.

From ancient Sumer, the laments of poets and singers still resonate with the agony of those who today suffer from war and its deprivations, a universal human experience that transcends one culture, belief, or ideology. Just over four thousand years ago, in what is modern-day Iraq, the ancient Sumerian city of Ur fell. Its poet(s) suggested that the Sumerians were abandoned by their gods to an enemy army from the east, which brought great suffering upon the people through no fault of their own. The Sumerian poet recites:

The Lamentation over the Destruction of Sumer and Ur

Who can oppose the commands of An and Enlil?
An frightened the (very) dwelling of Sumer, the people were
    afraid,
Enlil blew an evil storm, silence lay upon the city . . .
Revolt descended upon the land, something that no one had ever
    known,
Something unseen, which had no name, something that could
    not be fathomed.
The lands were confused in their fear,
The god of the city turned away, its shepherd vanished.
The people, in fear, breathed only with difficulty,

The storm immobilizes them, the storm does not let them
    return. . . .
The bright time was wiped out by a shadow.
On the bloody day, *mouths* were crushed, heads were crashed,
The storm was a harrow coming from above, the city was struck
    (as) by a hoe.
On the day, heaven rumbled, the earth trembled, the storm
    worked without respite,
The heavens were darkened, they were covered by shadow, the
    mountains roared,
The sun lay down at the horizon, dust *passed over* the mountains,
The moon lay at the zenith, the people were afraid. . . .
Large trees were being uprooted, the forest growth was ripped
    out,
The orchards were being stripped of their fruit,
they were being cleaned of their offshoots. . . .
[. . .] they piled up in heaps [. . .] they spread out like sheaves.
There were corpses (floating) in the Euphrates, brigands roamed
    [the roads]. . . .
The rich left his possessions and took an unfamiliar path. . . .
Its king sat immobilized in the palace, all alone . . .
The palace of his delight, he was crying bitterly.
The devastating flood was leveling (everything),
Like a great storm it roared over the earth, who could escape it?
. . . Mother Ba'u was lamenting bitterly . . .
"Alas, the destroyed city, my destroyed temple!" bitterly she
    cries. . . .
On the fields fine grains grew not, people had nothing to eat. . . .
Eridu, floating on great waters, *was deprived* of drinking water,
. . . its outer environs . . . turned into haunted places. . . ,
The loyal man in a place of treachery. . . .
In Ur no one went to fetch food, no one went to fetch drink,
Its people rush around like water *churning* in a well,
Their strength has ebbed away, they cannot (even) go on their
    way . . .
Its people, like fish being grabbed (in a pond) sought shelter,
Everyone lay spread about, no one could rise . . .

(As) the day grew dark, the eye (of the sun) was eclipsing, (the
    people) experienced hunger. . . .
The trees of Ur were sick, the reeds of Ur were sick,
Laments sounded all along its city wall.
Daily there was slaughter before it.
Large axes were sharpened in front of Ur,
The spears, the arms of battle, were being launched,
The large bows, javelin, and siege-shield gather together to strike,
The barbed arrows covered its outer side like a raining cloud. . . .
Daily the evil wind returns to (attack) the city.
Ur, which had been confident in its own strength, stood ready for
    slaughter,
Its people, oppressed by the enemy, could not withstand (their)
    weapons.
(Those) in the city who had not been felled by weapons, died of
    hunger,
Hunger filled the city like water, it would not cease,
(This) hunger contorts (people's) faces, it twists their muscles.
Its people are (as if) surrounded by water, they gasp for
    breath. . . .
"Alas, what can we say about it, what more can we add to it?
How long until we are finished off by (this) catastrophe?"
. . . In Ur (people) were smashed as if they were clay pots,
Its refugees were (unable) to flee, they were trapped inside the
    walls. . . .[2]
(from lines 57–129; 221–23; 293–305; 379–407)

No less compelling is *The Lamentation over the Destruction
of Ur*, with its graphic detail of human suffering and a haunting
refrain, thirty times over, "the people groan," "the people groan,"
"the people groan. . . ."[3] These are examples of communal laments
or dirges for a whole people, community, or nation, and this type
of literature is found across cultures. It is believed that in Sumer,
priests largely recited laments in rituals, but often in what is called
an *emesal* dialect; some believe this was a traditional dialect used by
women in their lament songs. Did women poets and singers compose some of these laments, along with men, that were then recited

by priests? This is a matter of scholarly debate, but the pervasive role of women singers of lament in other cultures, as well as the acceptance of women prophets in ancient Mesopotamia, is suggestive. Priests recited laments to commemorate a national tragic event, but also as part of a ritual when a temple was torn down in order to be rebuilt.

In sharing voices of lament from ancient times to the present, we hear not what some think of—an ever-cycling "clash of civilizations"—but rather, a shared human understanding: that *politically caused suffering* to the detriment of the masses is unacceptable in our interdependent *advance of cultures*. We can hear what that suffering has been like for those who came before us around the globe, for those around us today, and heaven help us, let us stop contributing to the suffering of our fellow human beings. Let us hear people's voices and lyrics, poignant and powerful in their languages and cultural colors, of their heartrending experience from their situations, as much as we can understand. Lament, in essence, provides a cathartic vehicle for human beings to express all aspects of suffering and to help maintain the value and dignity of one's humanity under hardship, if possible. Lament is, and not secondarily, a call to bring attention to injustice, an anguished plea for respite and consolation, an appeal for intervention not only to one's deity, but to one's community, and to the world community.

Enheduanna, the ancient Sumerian poet priestess, stands with many female poets and singers across cultures who struggled with the decimations of war and tragedy on family and community. Researcher Daniela Gioseffi recently refocused attention on her poem, "Lament to the Spirit of War." It probably dates to even earlier than the above Sumerian laments:

Lament to the Spirit of War

Enheduanna

You hack everything down in battle . . .
God of War, with your fierce wings
You slice away the land and charge
Disguised as a raging storm,

Growl as a roaring hurricane,
Yell like a tempest yells,
Thunder, rage, roar, and drum,
Expel evil winds!
Your feet are filled with anxiety!
On your lyre of moans
I hear your loud dirge scream.

Like a fiery monster you fill the land with poison.
As thunder you growl over the earth,
Trees and bushes collapse before you.
You are blood rushing down a mountain,
Spirit of hate, greed and anger,
Dominator of heaven and earth!
Your fire wafts over our land,
Riding on a beast,
With indomitable commands,
You decide all fate.
You triumph over all our rites.
Who can explain why you go on so?[4]

The Role of the Gods?

Enheduanna's lament, from about 4,300 years ago, shows how ancient peoples and cultures often attributed destructions of great magnitude to the intentions and actions of deities, not merely to human effort or foible with far-reaching effect. A certain god is on our side, or, our god is unhappy with us. How else might one explain the sheer force of destruction while also making sense of it? Some ancient singers and poets blame their own leaders or people for bringing on the devastation that represents the deity's displeasure or even punishment for their wrongdoing, yet other laments maintain the people's innocence. Laments were and remain embedded in socio-politico-historical contexts, while they also reach beyond with meanings for later listeners.

In many ancient cultures, kings could claim a share in divinity, that the deity's power was behind the leader's actions; occasionally kings could be corralled by a culture's ethical or legal code concerned for justice. The understanding of ancient Israel was that her kings were not divine and were to be guided by and serve Torah ethics, but they also did at times claim God's sanction. The prophets often corralled them and their power back to Torah ethics, with blistering critique. When modern presidents and prime ministers employ emotional national rhetoric to imply "God" is on their side to unleash or direct war, they are appealing to patriotism, but also they are participating in a practice as old as the hills—invoking divine approval for their human action. Like ancient leaders, they know that claimed divine sanction and sought-after victory produces a kind of magical effect, translating into their prestige and retention of power. Ancient laments of the people across cultures, however, are often more preoccupied with their suffering than with its cause. Today, people of faith from different religions might ask whether the deity or transcendent reality they follow really so favors "our nation" and "our people" in such a way as to wreak devastation on other peoples and nations and evoke their sad lament. Those who eschew "faith," on the other hand, often suggest that the faithful are always simply constructing "God" in their own image for self-interested ends against others. Surely many people find themselves wanting to follow a middle path between such extremes.

Interestingly, Enheduanna above was probably the daughter of King Sargon the Great, who conquered many peoples within a sizable empire. In her lament poem on war, she attributes *human* features and motives to the "God of War," crafting symbolic lyrics to render his power, with wings and feet, hacking and slicing, growling and screaming, riding on a beast, being hateful, greedy, and angry. People often create such apocalyptic-like images in laments to render the conditions of dire crisis or emergency, usually under horrible persecution. The beastlike Death, personified, is another feature of traditional lament poetry that we will see again later.

Is Enheduanna being sardonic by implying that there may be no difference between a male king and a god in their human, warring features? The end result is a poem that nearly personifies War itself to render the devastating effect upon her people; does it really matter if War is divine or human when people suffer so? Perhaps the gifted daughter of that king shook her head with realist insight and ironically recorded what appears to be *the first text in human history*, with an ending that still stands as a prophetic portent today: "Who can explain why you go on so?"!

Today, a Palestinian American poet performs a poem in which she vows that she will not participate in war.

What I Will

Suheir Hammad

I will not
dance to your war
drum. I will
not lend my soul nor
my bones to your war
drum. I will
not dance to your
beating. I know that beat.
It is lifeless. I know
intimately that skin
you are hitting. It
was alive once
hunted stolen
stretched. I will
not dance to your drummed
up war. I will not pop
spin break for you. I
will not hate for you or
even hate you. I will
not kill for you. Especially
I will not die
for you. I will not mourn
the dead with murder nor
suicide. I will not side
with you nor dance to bombs
because everyone else is

dancing. Everyone can be
wrong. Life is a right not
collateral or casual. I
will not forget where
I come from. I
will craft my own drum. Gather my beloved
near and our chanting
will be dancing. Our
humming will be drumming. I
will not be played. I
will not lend my name
nor my rhythm to your
beat. I will dance
and resist and dance and
persist and dance. This heartbeat is louder than
death. Your war drum ain't
louder than this breath.[5]

Women Singers Worldwide

Not only Enheduanna, but across the globe historically, women
have had to bear an inordinate share of the burden of war and
its aftermath, as warriors or soldiers return home debilitated, or
not at all. Women have been the victims of rape, and in some cultures, family members could be taken into slavery by the victor. In
many traditional cultures (though certainly not all), women were
called upon to sing or chant laments, usually dirge songs for the
dead. However, there is more than one instance in history where
women's public voices of lament were then deemed too socially
or politically influential or unacceptable by male leaders to be
allowed to continue their lament practice—classical Greece being
most notable, and also by some leaders of early Islam (see below).
These attempts did not completely prevent women from lamenting. In the case of Greece, women's laments were curtailed perhaps to limit the call for revenge, as well as women's influence in
the traditional clan social structure and its funerals where they had

a say about inheritance rights. The old clan system threatened to undermine the growing power of the emerging Greek polis or city-state, which curtailed women's rights and yet demanded greater socio-political loyalty.[6]

The *dirge* and the *lament prayer to the deity* are the two primary forms of lament across cultures and religions. Of course, they employ different terminologies, depending on the language and culture. In oral traditional cultures, whenever an individual in the community died, a local singer would compose a lament song for the deceased—a dirge—often simply by adapting existing phrases or crafting new lyrics for already familiar rhythms or tunes. One might pause and consider what it would be like today if every time someone died in the world (in wars, genocide, disease, other tragedy), a singer composed and publicly performed a song for that person. The world would have to stop and spend a lot more time listening to songs, moved by the anguish of individual losses so vast, perhaps less moved to violent revenge and more moved to gratitude for the gift of a life, in order to prevent such future loss.

In the Bible, there are very few dirges presented in their original funeral setting, and David's lament (below) is situated within a narrative. We will see how the biblical prophets utilized and transformed the dirge form in their judgment speeches of warning. However, a woman's voice is central to the expression of suffering in the biblical book of Lamentations (which might be termed a "communal dirge with lament prayer") that concerns the sixth-century B.C.E. destruction of Jerusalem, as well as the deaths, suffering, and exile of the Judeans to Babylon. We will return to this seminal text later, but here is an example of the singer's lament. Her words became a challenge to theological understandings of the time and to God, who was believed to have allowed the communal destruction as punishment.

> "O LORD, look at my affliction,
> For the enemy has triumphed!"
> . . . Look, O LORD, and see
> how worthless I have become.
> Is it nothing to you, all you who pass by?

Look and see if there is any sorrow like my sorrow
which was brought upon me,
which the LORD inflicted
on the day of his fierce anger. (Lam 1:9c, 11c-12)

Al-Khansa' (Tumadir bint 'Amr) was a famous woman poet in Bedouin culture of the sixth and seventh centuries C.E. in Arabia. Some of her lament lyrics preceded, and later witnessed to, Muhammad's influence and the rise of Islam; she composed dirges (or elegies called *rithā'* in Arabic), including for the deaths of her brothers, Sakhr and Muawiya, who died in tribal battles. Women used this genre for mourning laments. Al-Khansa' is regarded as the most accomplished of women Arabic poets of the era. More fluid and powerful in the original Arabic, this lament was composed for her brothers:

Allah Watered Earth that Came to Hold Them with the Morning Cloud's Downpour

I see time wasting my tribe, my father's sons.
I became tears that my weeping does not dry.
O Sakhr, what use is lament or grief
for the dead in a grave that was a halt?

Let not Allah remove Sakhr and his love
nor Allah remove my lord Muawiya.
Let Allah not displace Sakhr, for he is
brother of bounty building by high acts.

I will weep them, by Allah, while grief longs
and while Allah fixes the mountain peaks.
Allah watered earth that came to hold them
with the morning cloud's downpour.[7]

Al-Khansa' composed the above song after adopting Islam and invoking Allah ("God" in Arabic). She extolled those who were martyred in battle in the name of faith. In the first part of another elegy she personifies Death:

Elegy for My Brother

What have we done to you, death
that you treat us so,
with always another catch
one day a warrior
the next a head of state;
charmed by the loyal
you choose the best.
Iniquitous, unequalling death
I would not complain
if you were just,
but you take the worthy
leaving fools for us. . . .[8]

In early authoritative Muslim traditions—in parts of the *hadith* and *fiqh* (Muslim jurisprudence)—women were discouraged if not prohibited from participating in mourning over death, from loud wailing and possibly also from composing lyrics for the dead. This was to distinguish the religion from pre-Islamic practice, but one wonders if it were not also based on gender restriction due to the increasing authority of male religious leaders. As indicated above, Al-Khansá did not relinquish composing laments after she converted to Islam. In Iran, Afghanistan, and elsewhere, women's lament customs remain till today, including chanting laments by professional women and men mourners. In some traditional cultures, however, women are not allowed to attend the actual funeral rite/burial.[9]

A modern-day women's protest movement against war, death, and violence, Women in Black started in Jerusalem in 1988 when Jewish and Palestinian women stood together silently in public, wearing black, a sign of mourning.[10] Such women's protest movements inspire one another across cultures, including the Black Sash in South Africa and the Madres de la Plaza de Mayo in Argentina. Today these women, often mothers who have lost children, are living witnesses and symbols of women survivors over the millennia who have borne grievous losses and lamented across cultures. They have finally decided to protest silently what they have endlessly been called upon to lament. While all lament prayers, poems, or songs are "embodied" when spoken or performed, these women embody lament silently. Recently, the mothers among more than 160 families in China, who were protesting to the government over young people killed at Tiananmen Square, formed an organization seeking redress, the Tiananmen Mothers' Campaign. Biblical scholar Archie C. C. Lee wrote in 2004 that "after fourteen bitter years the authorities still deny these legitimate mourners and justified lamenters the possibility of public mourning and remembrance of the dead." Some have written poems, such as the anonymous one excerpted here:

Crying Over Child: To the Child Killed by Nine Gun Shots

3. Last night
Mum heard gunshots. In the blaze
Unarmed civilians,
Fallen one after another.
Then they brought you
Back in a stretcher.
At that time
You could no longer take a glance
At your Mum.
Just then you were still vivacious!
Toward Mum, you could still make
funny faces.
How come you've nine gun wounds in
your body?
Blood gushing out
All the way along High Street
To the courtyard!

4. They said you were a rioter,
They said
You'd sabotage the 20-million-lives-
built great palace.
Nevertheless
Mum knows

You were just a naïve child
Pulling Mum's hand yesterday
Urged Mum to take you to the park.[11]

While this book is focused primarily on vocal lament, much could be said about "embodied lament," for example, in those social justice leaders who are or were imprisoned or under house arrest for political dissidence, such as Nelson Mandela, Aung San Suu Kyi, Martin Luther King Jr., and others, and all those protesters in their movements imprisoned for their beliefs. Archbishop Desmond Tutu's Truth and Reconciliation Commission of South Africa made possible, in a public hearing, the embodied vocalizing of the people's laments and experience under the apartheid regime.

Laments for the Dead Inspiring Movements

The singing of dirges or laments to commemorate a lost hero (analogous to a spoken eulogy) can be institutionalized in a tradition to give inspiration to its adherents. For example, in Afghanistan, women have composed many poems and songs in memory of their martyred hero, Meena, who struggled for women's and human rights and democracy, through the Revolutionary Association of Women of Afghanistan (RAWA). This is especially important where women's very lives have been at great risk in exercising basic freedoms denied by some in power who made traditional culture extreme in its abrogation of human rights, and where even singing in recent years was banned by the Taliban. All such voicing is dangerous for those who utter it and a threat to those in power who are oppressing the people. Here is an example of one poem for Meena by Neesha Mirchandani, inspiring her followers.

Meena Lives within Us

MEENA: She is the beacon of hope within us
She shines the lantern into the darkness
She is the part of us that knows that tomorrow will be better,
    if we continue the struggle and spread the light.

She is the part of us that never gives up. . . .
She is in every RAWA action . . .
Every blanket distribution in every refugee camp.
In every school and every orphanage from Islamabad to Kandahar.
If the light of hope is in your heart, Meena is still alive.

MEENA: She is the voice of courage within us
She is not afraid of the power of the powerful
She is the part of us that speaks up with courage
She is the part of us that dispels a sea of despair. . . .
She is there when you travel to strange lands to tell your story.
If your voice of courage still can be heard, Meena is still in this
    world.

MEENA: She is the source of power within us
She is not ashamed to be a strong woman
She is the part of us that believes that women deserve equality
She is the part of us that refuses anything less
And claims her human rights without apologies. . . .

MEENA: She is the beauty within us
They murdered her beautiful body
But they couldn't silence Meena's voice
They couldn't take Meena's courage
They couldn't kill Meena's hope
They couldn't steal Meena's dream
Meena is in every RAWA member, in every RAWA song
She will never die as long as we believe in her vision
Meena lives eternally within us forevermore.[12]

A very significant example for Muslim tradition of an institutionalized lament for a spiritual martyr is the commemoration of
the tragic death of Imam Ḥusayn, grandson of Muhammad, and
other martyrs in Karbalā (present-day Iraq) in 680 C.E. Most important for Shi'ite Muslims in many cultures, honoring Imam Ḥusayn is
also practiced by some Sunnis, including Sufis, for example in Iran,
Turkey, and India, who have revered him as a model of piety and selfless suffering. Poets from all these traditions have composed lament

lyrics and mourning rituals of poignant devotion enacted every year in various countries during the first ten days of the month of Moḥarram, the first month of the Muslim lunar calendar year. Imam Ḥusayn is remembered especially on the tenth day, Ashura (Arabic; related to the Hebrew term ʿāsōr). Usually accompanied by the traditional ritual beating of the breast or the body as a sign of grief, this centuries-old Muslim lament tradition came to emphasize the practitioners' remorse, self-sacrifice, and expressions of mourning for Ḥusayn and others killed by a rival group. Sunnis also fast on this day, a practice adopted from the Jewish Day of Atonement (Yom Kippur) that also falls on the tenth day of the first month (Tishri) of the Jewish lunar calendar, and that emphasizes self-denial and forgiveness.[13]

Here is an example of an early lament for Imam Ḥusayn by his wife, Rabab. Most of these songs have a rhyme pattern and meter that is lost in English translation:

An Elegy for Ḥusayn

He who was a light, shining, is murdered;
Murdered in Karbalā, and unburied.
Descendant of the Prophet, may God reward you well;
May you be spared judgement on the day when deeds are
    weighed:
For you were to me as a mountain, solid, in which I could take
    refuge;
And you treated us always with kindness, and according to
    religion.
O who shall speak now for the orphans, for the petitioners;
By whom shall all these wretched be protected, in whom shall
    they take refuge?
I swear by God, never will I wish to exchange marriage with you
    for another;
No, not until I am covered; covered in the grave.[14]

Laments take the form of *marthiya* (Arabic),[15] lament poems that had their origins in pre-Islamic times, usually performed by women. They were a type of the Arabic *qasida* poem. A *marthiya* describes the positive qualities of the deceased and the losses to the mourner. This poetic tradition has lasted for 1,400 years in Islam, but has no parallel in Christian tradition, except for the honoring of the martyrs in the church calendar. A *marthiya* could include a call for revenge if there was a perpetrator of the death, who might also be cursed.[16] In the Ashura ritual commemoration for Imam Ḥusayn, a lead singer might chant a dirge (*nauha/nawḥa*), or recite from a written *maqtal* (a narrative of what happened). These can be in various languages (Arabic, Urdu, Turkish, Persian, Hindi), depending on the culture and country; in Iran there is a short *mosibat* oral form of lament, rendering episodes of the affliction of Ḥusayn and other martyrs that can evoke mourning and tears from the participants. Some great poets, including the Qajar poets of Persia/Iran, and other spiritual leaders, composed a myriad of such laments, varying throughout history, that recount such suffering.[17]

Additional elements of the Ashura ritual during medieval times when the community gathered, and a number of customs that have carried over to today, include public sermons, burial rituals, a parade of coffins, pageantry, theater, and self-mortification processions including beating one's chest (*matam*) or back. This is an ancient mourning custom related to that found in the Bible. For example, Luke's Gospel records such a custom at Jesus' crucifixion: "When all the crowds who had gathered there for this spectacle saw what had taken place, they returned home, beating their breasts" (Luke 23:48). However, the Ashura ritual also is a purposeful, prolonged self-identification with the sufferer through repetitive self-flagellation, which for some even draws blood.[18]

Other practices for Ashura can include storytelling about the suffering of Ḥusayn's mother Fāṭema, his sister Zaynab, his wife Bibi, and the tragic fate of Ḥusayn's sons; but also some joyous, carnival-like celebration has come to be mixed in with the mourning. While some find repulsive the occasionally extreme form of ritual violence against one's body, most religious traditions contain some form of such ascetic practices that seek a spiritual state of union with a martyr or God. The Ashura tradition also provides what has been called the "Karbalā paradigm," in which those who feel oppressed take comfort from Ḥusayn's experience for their own suffering due to political tyranny or injustice by oppressors. The tradition can inspire revolution, and raises the question again of the role of lament in relation to violence. Among the Sufis (and most Muslims), Ḥusayn is revered as a model of suffering, of love and self-sacrifice, and is also revered by some as a model of someone willing to fight and die in the pursuit of God's will and glory over against the world's wrongs.[19]

Here is part of another lament for Ḥusayn by the poet Jafar b. 'Affan (from the Ummayid period, 651–750 c.e.), probably composed at a gathering of members of Muhammad's family:

Lament for Ḥusayn

He who weeps for Ḥusayn might well weep for Islam itself,
For the principles of Islam have been destroyed, and used
　　unlawfully:
On the day when Ḥusayn became the target of spears,
When swords drank from him, busy with their work.
And corpses, scattered, were abandoned in the desert.
Great birds hovering over by night and by day. . . .[20]

Irshaad Hussain describes a typical Ashura ritual with lament singing in Canada today:

The men arranged themselves in long loose lines facing each other—the younger ones . . . moved to the front lines and faced off against each other. One of the older men, wearing a long black traditional kurta, in a powerful voice began to recite a rhythmical, tuneful chant (a *nauha*). And as his voice rose and fell, singing out in heart rending verse the story of Ḥusayn's sacrifice at Karbala, the men began to beat their breasts, pounding out a steady rhythmic accompaniment to the verses on their flesh. Their "matam" (breast beating) began slowly, gingerly, then gradually strengthened, settling into a steady metronomic beat. A dramatic, affecting aura settled over the hall, strengthened by the hammering heartbeat like pulse of the matam.

The reciter's voice rose to a peak on the chorus. The others joined their voices to that of the reciter's on the refrain, and a sea of arms flew up and pounded downwards onto waiting chests—repeatedly—with shuddering force. . . . The reciter was singing out—his voice breaking as it strained to keep pace with the steady deep thumping of the breast beaters. "Allah Kya jigar tha janabe Ḥusayn ka"—"O God, what a heart this Ḥusayn had!" Men wept openly—their faces wet with tears—anguished cries rang out and echoed in the hall so that one could almost imagine that the martyrdom of Ḥusayn was unfolding right there, right then, in that hall. Wet eyes gazed into the distance—as if staring out at the scene described in the reciter's verses—their hearts breaking on Ḥusayn's behalf. Such an atmosphere of sorrow filled the hall—an air of heightened spirituality but one laden with heartbreak at the direction Ḥusayn's submission to God was forced to take.

As one reciter ended his "nauha," another would step in to take over. The tunes fluctuated in intensity and tempo, and the force of the "matam"—the breast beating—ebbed and flowed with the changing rhythms. These "nauhas" pulsed with a magnetic force—their sad melodies, their achingly beautiful words and powerful beat drumming out Ḥusayn's drama of self-sacrifice, absolute commitment, and egoless devotion. . . . Here in this hall, another plane of reality arose on the drumbeat of chests and the lamenting cries of Ḥusayn, Ḥusayn. Time was briefly erased as the magnitude of the matam and the absolute concentration of the mourners evoked the memory of the final moments of the martyrs of Karbala. . . . Outside, on the wintery streets, cars ploughed through the snow and slush of Canada's roads.[21]

Various topics of lament among contemporary Muslim poets are found in the "spoken word" of Suheir Hammad, Brother Dash, and the poetry of Daniel Abdal-Hayy Moore. One poem laments and poignantly corrects misunderstandings about Islam.

Headline Islam

The air above the horizon tremors
As the warmth of our hearts rise above the raging waters of
    turmoil
And chaos humanity breeds
We be the lighthouses with spiritual beacons standing stoic never
    changed by the

Spray of salty voices that clap against our bedrock foundation
We sing sweet soft somethings so succulent some suckle several
    sips
We cradle the young we sit silent before the veteran and
We open the curtains for sun rays to destroy the darkness and we
    pull wool blankets over the bodily flaws of our companions
    shielding them from sight.
We be the torchbearers following straight paths of guided light
Struggling as we lead the masses through 34 prostrations as the
    day passes
Grass is growing 'cause even the scorched Earth be knowing that
    we be rain water
Healing Bani Adam's slaughter
Bringing order not verbal mortars
Teaching daughters not to be porters
To men who grin getting drunk of Jinn
Spelled J-I-N-N
10 to the 10, 10 be the power of this verse by verse
First nurse those who feel cursed
Squeeze those who feel worse
And touch and soothe and kiss the hearts in tribulation 'cause
    we all got the same destination
And too many of us are getting left at every Hip-Hop and R&B
    station
Mira Nosotros somos hermanos you see these manos?
They fight for you,
Stay tight for you,
In several hues
Red, Black, Brown and yeah White too
So don't twist your wrist this kiss be Jennah bliss
Get my drift?
We uplift our palms 45 degrees Be pleased
'Cause we drownin' in the herbal teas of mu'min energies
That breeze puttin' you at mental ease?
Contains the moisture from honey melon seas
Forming liquid beads

Whose seeds bleed the nectar formed from compassionate
    wisdom
Taste the sweetness on your lips
Then grip the tips
Of your modern day quills
Be scribes at will and drill
These words into heart stones where dreams moan
And bellies groan from a hunger and a thirst
For a spiritual elixir
610 was a very good year HEAR!
The cries of their fears
Make wudhu in Kaffir tears
Why?
'Cause your salvation ain't in condemnations
or exhortations of eternal damnation
According to the level of your mental maturation
It be in boats filled with Haitians
Po' White Mamas in the Appalachians
Milk carton photo shoots
Similac minds in high stiletto boots
Paper Mache gods made from disposable agendas
Burnt out converts who said RETURN TO SENDER
Grab your flag Shahadatayn be your refrain
But don't refrain
There's too much pain
Let's wash these stains
With celestial rain
With celestial rain
Our passion is compassion
So release and share
Smiles are hugs
Words are kisses
So what's a touch but a prelude to hearts that join in spiritual
    remembrance
That serenade a love supreme
That cry serendipitous tears not saline but clear
Zam Zam for the human mind

So in times of defining moments in this moment define
    yourselves
Tell your own stories
Sing your own psalms
Re-Write the headline
Saying NO! *THIS* be Islam.[22]

Poets and singers worldwide, whether famous or not, both men and women, often compose dirges for leading figures, expressing the felt loss of many people, even a nation, especially when the leaders and their ideals have been slain by malicious wrong. Take, for example, this famous dirge for Abraham Lincoln:

O Captain! My Captain!

Walt Whitman

O Captain! my Captain! our fearful trip is done,
The ship has weather'd every rack, the prize we sought is won,
The port is near, the bells I hear, the people all exulting.
While follow eyes the steady keel, the vessel grim and daring;
    But O heart! heart! heart!
      O the bleeding drops of red,
        Where on the deck my Captain lies,
          Fallen cold and dead.

O Captain! my Captain! rise up and hear the bells;
Rise up—for you the flag is flung—for you the bugle trills,
For you bouquets and ribbon'd wreaths—for you the shores
    a-crowding,
For you they call, the swaying mass, their eager faces turning;
    Here Captain! dear father!
      This arm beneath your head!
        It is some dream that on the deck,
          You've fallen cold and dead.

My Captain does not answer, his lips are pale and still,
My father does not feel my arm, he has no pulse nor will,
The ship is anchor'd safe and sound, its voyage closed and done,

From fearful trip the victor ship comes in with object won;
> Exult O shores, and ring O bells!
>> But I with mournful tread,
>>> Walk the deck my Captain lies,
>>>> Fallen cold and dead.[23]

Whitman's much lengthier dirge for Lincoln, "When Lilacs Last in the Dooryard Bloom'd," was later adapted for a musical composition by the German composer Paul Hindemith, commissioned for performance by Robert Shaw, to honor Franklin D. Roosevelt upon his death and the Americans who fought in World War II. Hindemith and his wife, who was Jewish, had to flee Germany in the 1930s; his music either fell in disfavor with or had been banned by Hitler.[24]

The lament poem "Elegy" by A.M. Klein, cited earlier, expressed the difficulty of Shoah survivors in lamenting so many persons lost. The years when millions were still in camps facing their own imminent deaths was an unspeakable time of lamenting. Here are a few examples of lament songs, including translations, as found on the United States Holocaust Memorial Museum website, where the reader can listen. The first is sung by historian Joseph Wulf, who was in an Auschwitz labor camp and helped arrange concerts for inmates. Though his lament "Sunbeams" (1943) hopes for freedom (and Wulf was liberated in 1945), nearly thirty years later he took his own life after despairing that the German authorities were not cooperating with his efforts to tell the full history.

Sunbeams

Joseph Wulf

Sunbeams, radiant and warm,
Human bodies, young and old;
And we who are imprisoned here,
Our hearts are yet not cold.
Souls afire, like the blazing sun,
Tearing, breaking through their pain,
For soon we'll see that waving flag,
The flag of freedom yet to come.

White snow falling, silent, lonely,
On this dark and dreadful world;
And we who are imprisoned here,
Are wakeful as the stars at night.
Souls afire, like the blazing sun,
Tearing, breaking through their pain,
For soon we'll see that waving flag,
The flag of freedom yet to come.[25]

From Auschwitz, as well, is a Romani Gypsy lament song called
"Auschwitz," also on this website:

Auschwitz

Anonymous

And at Auschwitz there is a big prison.
There sits my lover,
He sits, he sits, and thinks,
He forgets me.
You, black bird,
Take a letter for me,
Go to my friend, to my wife,
Tell her I am at Auschwitz.
At Auschwitz there is a great famine,
There is nothing to eat,
What is there? just a piece, a small piece of bread—
And the guard there is evil.[26]

More recently in the United States, for the two tragic deaths
of 1968 and for fallen heroes before, Dick Holler composed a song
performed by the singer Dion, a type of communal dirge for the
nation's losses. It became the most popular song of the 1960s in the
United States.

Abraham, Martin, and John

Anybody here seen my old friend Martin?
Can you tell me where he's gone? . . .[27]

Many laments were composed by Indian poets and singers for Mahatma Gandhi upon his heartbreaking assassination, yet they are rare in English translation. Surely they would be an inspiration to many around the world for this immensely beloved leader.[28]

Such influential figures live on, and the more famous the person, the more lasting the song, as was David's biblical lament for King Saul and Jonathan:

> Saul and Jonathan, beloved and lovely!
> In life and in death they were not divided;
> they were swifter than eagles,
> they were stronger than lions.
> O daughters of Israel, weep over Saul. . . . (2 Sam 1:23-24a)

The outpouring of grief by people around the world at the occasion of Princess Diana's funeral revealed something of the universal human need to process loss through ritual. A tribute song, a dirge really, newly rendered by Elton John and Bernie Taupin and based on "Candle in the Wind,"[29] was a poignant reworking, a modern-day "oral tradition" for a new context.

More recently, Elton John and Bernie Taupin composed a lament song, "American Triangle," as a tribute to Matthew Shepard, a young gay man who was murdered in the state of Wyoming in a hate crime in 1998. He was brutally beaten and left tied to a fence. The case brought national attention to the injustice and inhumanity of hate crimes and discrimination against persons in the United States who are homosexual.[30]

Apart from well-known figures, what would it mean if there were a return to the ancient practice of composing a song whenever someone died, and performing it in neighborhood gathering places or religious communities? At recent workshops in U.S. culture, religious leaders, music leaders, and everyday folks were asked to contemplate this where the custom has been lost. In a simple, poignant activity of each of them remembering a loved one they'd lost, and aspects of their personality, they began creating a simile or image that reflected that person (following the example of how the lyrics of "Candle in the Wind" were transformed for Diana). They began to compose lyrics quite naturally. They were able to set their lyrics to the tune of the remembered person's favorite song. One woman bravely undertook the task for her mother, who had died just six months prior. She composed beautiful song lyrics, though she had never done so in her life. And though it grieved her too much to sing them, she read them, and those listening were blessed by entering into the personal expressions of grief, a healing gift. She confessed that the composing, then and over time, had been a welcome help and truly transformative for attending to her sorrow and restoring her life. Yet, such a natural process, a living dynamic of creating songs, was once a part of traditional cultures that has been tragically lost in much of the West and its communities of faith. What would it mean to restore such a living process to communities, or to include them in public rituals?

Death and tragedy—for individuals, local communities, and nations—have produced laments worldwide. In the next chapter, we turn more to the laments themselves and the traditional features they often exhibit.

---∞∞∞---

━━━━━━━━━━━━━━━ ⟨∞∞⟩ ━━━━━━━━━━━━━━━

CHAPTER TWO

Features of "Traditional" Lament across Cultures

Comparisons of lament traditions from around the globe, of folks expressing their sorrow and suffering, reveal beautiful distinctions as well as shared features. Let us begin with the *process of lament composition and singing* itself—that is, the living dynamic of popular, oral traditional singing. This communal process is diminishing but is still found worldwide where close-knit village, rural, or small-town communities, and their shared spaces and customs, have not yet been fragmented and displaced politically, industrially, or by globalizing developments. Great intentionality is now needed to preserve or restore communities' oral traditional processes, including lament. In this process, gifted individuals compose songs using formulaic phrases, rhythms, and patterns passed down through the generations from their cultural heritage, yet infuse the composition with their individual creativity in response to the immediate needs of the situation. In this kind of process, the composer of the lyrics *is also the performer/singer* (which is not always the case in modern cultures). Traditional oral poetic singers employ folk and/or religious ritual practices. Of course, written literary laments may also include traditional motifs.

While the process is "traditional," there is a built-in mechanism for innovation and the improvisation of forms and ideas, and here is a great potential, a critical moment, for the introduction of progressive social or educational ideas that may challenge certain unhelpful ideas from the past. For example, people's understandings of the cause of AIDS-related death can be informed and corrected through funeral rituals in traditional communities, through the lyrics of dirge songs, lament prayers, and the words of homilies—to overturn destructive superstition, stigmatizing, and misinformation, and to alleviate fear and stop the persecution of persons living with AIDS.

The process of composing or performing traditional laments is relational. Usually children learn from individual mentors in the older generation. In the early 1900s, M. Murko, A. B. Lord, and M. Parry undertook groundbreaking field research in Yugoslavia on such an oral poetic process (on epic poetry performed in the community by men), in both Muslim and Christian cultures. Researchers around the world have documented similar composing and performing processes, including, for example, among Arab women singers in the 1980s (including for Christian, Muslim, and Druze cultures) in Galilee and the Golan Heights. Mishael Caspi and Julia Ann Blessing recorded laments there, and one woman described the practice:

> My grandmother was a eulogizer and my mother learned from her. When my mother was at home alone and remembered a member of her family who had passed away, she sang sorrowfully and mournfully about them. I learned these poems from her, and those who come after me will learn from me.[1]

Often an individual composes a poem or song by listening to others sing, whether in communal settings or at home privately, and then performs her or his own lyrics in the community. Another feature of laments suggested by this process is that they usually express *the voice of the people*, whose folk traditions also then bring along sacred meanings and/or infuse sacred rituals.

Bernice Johnson Reagon, a civil rights activist, has both performed (in the group Sweet Honey in the Rock) and taught the spirituals and gospel songs of the early black church traditions in the United States to several generations of people, young and old, in order to keep alive the tradition that was so instrumental in the success of the movement. Not only must the songs and the repertoire of lament be remembered and sung in communities and churches, but also the process of individuals' composing, improvising, and performing songs must be honored, particularly in the call-and-response mode of the community gathered. In oral tradition, every performance is a "new song," even though it is often an old, familiar song performed or arranged with "newness."[2]

Another traditional feature of laments is their *dialogical dimension*—that is, often the singing involves a lead singer with other singers who respond to a line or half-line with a refrain. These multiple voices are not always as apparent in a written literary lament as in an oral performance. This "call-and-response" element has been documented in performances of lament around the world. What is it that makes this style so universal and lasting, down through the millennia? Perhaps it is *community itself*, sharing the grief, which makes for a natural flow of multiple voices and overflow of emotion. It is healthier than sorrowing in isolation. There is someone else's response to one's expression of suffering, someone who comforts and resonates with the pain, and a "village" or community that shares the burden. The call and response of a lament song also can allow for improvisation as a creative, cathartic element in the expression. Scholars have recently begun taking more note of the dialogical element within the biblical psalms, and the different perspectives of the singers in what they express, especially with regard to the one who laments, and how another, or one representing God, responds to his or her suffering.[3] Dialogue does not reflect the individualism typical of the modern West, but rather reflects the community and different individual voices held together in the traditional process of singing. Improvisation is especially evident in the ancient singing of the psalms, including laments, of the synagogue,[4] as well as in more recent historic singing in black church traditions. Chapter 4 will attend further to these traditions.

Another feature of laments across cultures is that they usually fall within one of *two genres*: dirges (funeral songs) or lament prayers. Dirge performances may yet contain within them lament prayer to God. The dirge poems, and other funeral and mourning rituals and subsequent commemorations, provide needed avenues for processing grief. Some of the associated ritual actions and traditions practiced as part of mourning for the dead will vary across cultures, or even in one culture over time, but some typical actions include tearing one's clothes, wearing mourning garments, mourning with head and/or feet bare, throwing dust on the head, shearing one's hair, fasting, beating the breast or practice of self-injury, being in a posture on the ground, and having the bereaved provided with food, a feast, bread, or drink by the comforters.

Shared motifs in dirge songs across cultures reflect the common experiences of human suffering and, whether in traditional songs or in literary poems, can include the following: mention of a *death* and possibly how a person died, especially if it was due to violence or the unexpected; a *complaint* about the death and associated destruction, if any, often accompanied by *weeping*; *melancholy* over the transitoriness of the deceased/destroyed; a *contrast motif* (comparing "then and now"); sometimes an *accusation*, if there was a killer or attacker; sometimes a call for *justice, revenge, or a curse*; a *call-and-response* performance style that allows for different singers/speakers; direct *address of the dead*, or the dead speaking; *questions*; a *summons* to mourn; mourning over the *incomprehensibility* of the event; a statement about the *impact* of the death and/or destruction on the survivors; a *reconciling motif* (a "making peace" for the survivors with their loss by the fact that the individual's death was brave or noble, the burial honorable, leaving an honorable memory and a good name); *praise* for the deceased; and occasionally a *prayer* to the deity that may include a plea or expressions of hope.[5] As researchers of grief and trauma suggest, such verbal articulations of grief are likely to occur at a stage later than the initial shock of numbed silence.

Here are illustrations of some of these motifs. First, the singer or poet's *weeping* can be found in either the traditional dirge or the lament prayer, or may stand alone in a poem or song. The prophet Jeremiah, notable for his personal suffering, powerful poetry, laments, and warnings to Judah, composed these lyrics in the context of the sixth-century B.C.E. destruction of Jerusalem and the devastation of his people:

> O that my head were a spring of water,
> And my eyes a fountain of tears,
> That I might cry day and night
> For the slain Bat-'Ammî ['daughter of my people']. (Jer 9:1)[6]

> But if you will not listen
> my soul will weep in secret
> for your pride;
> my eyes will weep bitterly and
> run down with tears,
> because the LORD's flock has
> been taken captive. (Jer 13:17)

> Let my eyes run down with tears
> night and day
> and let them not cease,
> for the maiden Bat-'Ammî
> is struck down
> with a crushing blow,
> with a very grievous wound. (Jer 14:17)

The following example, which is reminiscent of Jeremiah's lyric and of Psalm 55, is from the well-known Croatian poet Jure Kaštelan, in the post–World War II context:

> My eyes today are as hundreds of springs,
> my voice a whistling wind from the glen.
> If only my arms were wings above the village
> that I might fly and fly, fly without cease.[7]

Of course, these examples are a poignant representative drop in the bucket of the lamenting that actually happens in enormous tragedy. Historically, the Shoah (Holocaust) and World War II are beyond compare for the size and extent of the suffering and losses, though preceded by the Armenian genocide earlier in the century. Rather than giving just one or a few expressions from the Shoah, let the reader imagine and, in the space and silence below, pay respect to the suffering of six million Jews, and the twenty million individuals altogether, who were killed, and let us add our silence of respect for the weeping of the twenty-five million people who have died of AIDS since 1981, for the victims of genocide in Armenia, Cambodia, Rwanda, Bosnia-Herzegovina, Sudan, and the Democratic Republic of the Congo, and the loved ones of all these who still grieve around the world.

Biblical Job is one of the classic figures who expresses his weeping as he pours out lament, but only after the book implies his initial stage of shock and denial. He identifies with innocent Abel, whose blood cried out from the ground.

> My face is red with weeping,
> and deep darkness is on my eyelids,
> though there is no violence in my hands,
> and my prayer is pure.
>
> O earth, do not cover my blood;
> Let my outcry find no resting place . . .
> My friends scorn me;
> my eye pours out tears to God. . . . (Job 16:16-18, 20)

Job is a literary figure, perhaps rooted in a historical figure, who is depicted as losing his children. If we may say so, the Palestinian doctor whose heartrending lament from Gaza was mentioned at the opening of this book, also lost, like so many others—both Israelis and Palestinians—their precious children by violent means. In all these, laments for the deaths of loved ones alternate readily with anguished prayers to God for help.

The lament below also joins these actions—weeping for a death and fervent appeal to God—here by an anonymous Israeli Arab woman, recorded by Mishael Caspi and Julia Ann Blessing in the early 1980s.

> O tears of my eyes, flow forth
> Renew your lament
> For the separation of the brother, weep
> O my brother, close to my heart
> Ah my brother, my beloved
> This is life's destiny
> God will diffuse my grief for me
> And teach me patience in this grievous time
> Ah (the) tears of my heart
> News of your death was broadcast
> Let us entreat God's mercy
> There is no escape from the pursuit of death.[8]

To lament one death or several is a most difficult experience. To lament the loss of an entire people is another. The Yiddish poet Jacob Glatstein lamented the countless Jews lost in the Holocaust:

Nightsong

In the dark I see shining towards me
faces of epitaphs
wailing their song. . . .[9]

As mentioned earlier, *personification* is a feature of traditional oral poetry and lament, and is carried over into written literary laments, including the personification of a nation, village, or city, of death and other realities, or of nature and inanimate structures. Sometimes this is linked to weeping and mourning, where nature and buildings, for example, themselves grieve.

It is well-known that the Hebrew biblical prophets personify Israel, Judah, and Jerusalem in their powerful lyrics, as well as other ancient countries and capital cities. Such personification by the prophets works in their poetry to console, judge, and warn the leaders and people, depending on the context. It is safe to say that one of the most distinctive contributions of the Hebrew biblical prophets, and of ancient Israel, was not only their pursuit of monotheism (extraordinary for its time), but especially the frank and open willingness to be self-critical, nationally and individually, according to the standards of the Torah, its ethics, and loyalty to the one God. Most people know that this prophetic tradition has continued to influence other religions and world cultures and their leaders for three thousand years, by suggesting that the well-being and even existence of a people is contingent upon its doing right. For example, the earliest prophet to whom we have a whole book attributed, Amos, used a "communal" dirge lament form in which he personified the northern kingdom of Israel, anticipating its death, its collapse, if it did not live up to the Torah:

Hear this word that I take up over you in lamentation, O house
of Israel:

Fallen, no more to rise,
is maiden Israel;

forsaken on her land,
with no one to raise her up . . .

. . . because you trample on the poor
and take from them levies of grain,
you have built houses of hewn stone,
but you shall not live in them . . .
For I know how many are your transgressions,
and how great are your sins—
you who afflict the righteous
who take a bribe,
and push aside the needy in the gate.

Therefore thus says the LORD . . .
in all the squares there shall be wailing;
and in all the streets they shall say "Alas! Alas!"
They shall call the farmers to mourning,
and those skilled in lamentation, to wailing. . . . (Amos 5:1-2,
    11-12, 16)

While in the 1990s the world watched and listened to the sad destruction of Sarajevo, very few people ever heard her personified laments rendered by her poets:

Planet Sarajevo

Abdulah Sidran

Listen
To the breathing
of Planet Sarajevo.

Listen
To the Girl crying:
"Death, don't take me along!"

How many times have we
Uttered
With tears
Our ardent prayers for peace?

Death cares not for the girl's tears,
Death cares not for human prayers. . . . [10]

Also from Bosnia-Herzegovina, the following poem excerpt exhibits personification to powerful effect, as a consolation to the people of a suffering town.

Mostar, the Vukovar of Herzegovina

Marija Koprivnjak

To Mostar—my beloved town . . .
The dark clouds of war,
destruction and decay have covered you . . .
The beautiful spring in you is now cloaked in black.
It weeps, moans, and sobs.[11]

Archie C. C. Lee analyzed a sixth century C.E. Chinese poem by a survivor of the defeat of the southern Liang country by Western Wei in the north. A characteristic of the overall poem depicts nature giving portents as warnings to leaders of wrongdoing; in this selection, personified nature participates in the devastation, as in the Bosnian lament above, here with a displaced people moving as exiles across their country:

Lament for the South

Yu Xin

A vengeful frost fell in summer;
Angry springs boiled up in autumn.
Qi's wife brought down a wall by her cries;
The Ladies of the Xiang stained bamboo with their tears.
Rivers poisonous as the streams of Qin,
Mountains as high as the range of Xing,
Ten miles, five miles,
Long halts, short halts,
Driven by hunger after hibernating swallows (lines 433–39).[12]

Personification of nature lamenting is also found in the Bible. For example, in Isaiah's apocalyptic vision in chapter 24, nature's processes and the earth itself are damaged by human wrong, and they mourn:

The earth dries up and withers,
the world languishes and withers;
the heavens languish together with the earth.
The earth lies polluted under its inhabitants;
for they have transgressed laws,
violated the statutes,
broken the everlasting covenant. . . .

The wine dries up,
the vine languishes,
all the merry-hearted sigh.
The mirth of the timbrels is stilled,
the noise of the jubilant has ceased,
The mirth of the lyre is stilled. . . .

The earth is utterly broken,
the earth is torn asunder,
the earth is violently shaken,
The earth staggers like a drunkard . . .
its transgression lies heavy upon it,
and it falls, and will not rise again. . . .

On that day, the LORD will punish
the host of heaven in heaven,
and on earth the kings of the earth . . .
Then the moon will be abashed,
and the sun ashamed. . . . (Isa 24:4-5, 7-8, 19-21, 23a)

While it is typical for commentators to speak of the poet's "personification" of nature, and even denigrate this practice as "primitive," let us suggest that there was far more to this than simply a literary device or unsophisticated understanding. These texts suggest a belief in the spiritual energies and personae within nature, whose source is God, yet who is separate; this is typical of other traditional cultures, and theologians call it panentheism. In a later passage, the prophet Isaiah conveys nature—the mountains and the land—as grieving in response to war, and God's judgment against ancient Assyria for attacking Israel:

Listen! The valiant cry in the streets;
the envoys of peace weep bitterly.
The highways are deserted,
travelers have quit the road.
The treaty is broken,
its oaths are despised,
its obligation is disregarded.
The land mourns and languishes;
Lebanon is confounded and withers away;
Sharon is like a desert;
and Bashan and Carmel shake off their leaves. (Isa 33:7-9)

There is something poignant and universal about this phenomenon, for it appears in laments in poetry, song, and sacred texts across cultures. For example, here is a Native American perspective:

Some day the earth will weep,
she will beg for her life,
she will cry with tears of blood.
You will make a choice,
if you will help her or let her die,
and when she dies, you too will die.[13]
—*John Hollow Horn*, Oglala Lakota

While Enheduanna, in her poem above, personified war, al-Khansa' personified death. The mourning women in the southern kingdom of Judah personify death as a "being" in the biblical book of Jeremiah:

Death has come up into our windows,
it has entered our palaces,
to cut off the children from the streets
and the young men from the squares. (Jer 9:21)

Hosea, an earlier biblical prophet of the eighth century B.C.E., had also personified death:

Shall I ransom them from the power of Sheol?
Shall I redeem them from Death?

O Death, where are your thorns?
O Sheol, where is your sting? (Hos 13:14)[14]

The prophet Isaiah also personified death:

The LORD of hosts will swallow up death forever,
Then the LORD God will wipe away the tears from all faces . . .
   (Isa 25:8a)

Following the practice of the prophets, the apostle Paul in the New Testament, who usually wrote prose, draws upon a longstanding tradition of personifying death when he reuses the poetry above to help him describe the resurrection of Jesus Christ and humanity.

Death has been swallowed up in victory.
O death, where is your victory, O Death where is your sting?
   (1 Cor 15:55)[15]

This lyric personifying Death is retained in the modern hymn "Christ the Lord Is Risen Today."

Another traditional feature of the dirge song or poem is the *contrast motif*, a comparison of life as it once was to what it is now, after the death of a person or the devastation of an entire community/nation. The biblical book of Lamentations reflects such a contrast after the destruction of Jerusalem in the sixth century B.C.E.

How the gold has grown dim,
how the pure gold is changed!
The sacred stones tumble down
at the head of every street;
The precious children of Zion,
worth their weight in fine gold—tossed aside.
How they are reckoned as broken pottery,
the work of a potter's hands! . . .
The tongue of the infant clings
to the roof of its mouth for thirst;
the children ask for bread;
no one is disbursing it to them.
Those who feasted on delicacies

perish in the streets;
those who were brought up in purple
cling to ash heaps. (Lam 4:1-2, 4-5)[16]

In another selection from his long poem "Elegy," cited in the previous chapter, A. M. Klein rendered the contrast of life as it once was for Jews in Europe and as it is after the Holocaust:

> . . . A world is emptied. Marked is that world's map
> The forest colour. There where Thy people praised
> In angular ecstasy Thy name, Thy Torah
> Is less than a whisper of its thunderclap.
> Thy synagogues, rubble . . . academies,
> Bright once with Talmud brow and musical
> With song alternative in exegesis,
> Are silent, dark. They are laid waste, Thy cities,
> Once festive with thy fruit-full calendar,
> And where Thy curled and caftan'd congregations
> Danced to the first days and the second star,
> Or made the marketplaces loud and green
> To welcome the Sabbath Queen;
> . . . there is nothing, nothing. . . .[17]

A Palestinian poet writes of the grievous changes to his village that was occupied and destroyed in 1948, and its inhabitants removed.

Trip in the Ruins of Al-Walaja

Mustafa Khalil al-Sayfi

> I'm thirsty . . . Where are the springs and wells?
>   Nothing, only wasteland and desert,
> Nothing but murky wilderness
>   The earth of the fields covered in stones.
> Where is "al-Dhuhur" of almond buds
>   And the "Hadayif" surrounded by wildflowers
> Where are the fields and birds of "al-Khalayil"
>   And "Wadi Ahmad," the grounds of the partridges

Where is "al-Hina" and its flowing water
    Its shade sheltering resting travelers
Where are the guests who suddenly appear
    And in the "Quffeh" the coals are lit [to cook for them]
So that in every house the men clash
    Like a huge wave, opening the way for a tornado
As a result of their love for the guests. . . .[18]

This poem not only poignantly laments the destruction and complete loss of the village by contrasting the remembered past to the present, but the "ruins" motif reflects another layer of meaning from Arabic cultural history. The genre *al-atlal* ("the ruins") has been used in classical Arabic love poetry since the pre-Islamic period, in which the surviving lover visits the abandoned places of his past life and laments the absence there of his beloved.[19]

The contrast motif shapes this excerpt of a poem that depicts the Croatian town of Vukovar, devastated by war in the 1990s; it had also been devastated in World War II.

Vukovar

Slavica Crnjac

In the old town of Vukovar
there was a sweet smell of lime-trees . . .
beautiful lime-trees fell,
"tambura" were silenced.[20]

Similarly, a poet of Sarajevo rendered the contrast after war's devastation in the 1990s, also using personification of the city and its buildings, and including a lament prayer, in this excerpt:

Record of the City in Blank Verse

Ljubica Ostojić

. . . in the City, those still living
reject the consolation of history
where everything gets repeated.
The City watches sadly

the freshly drawn omens of destiny:
unplanned new graveyards
wherever the beast had trod,
having come from its infernal darkness.
The City full of hollow silence:
with just the church bells shivering
and the wounded minarets
speaking quietly with the heaven,
pianos in the shattered chambers.
And the wind howls among the trees,
inside the broken statues,
inside the cracked, gray tombstones.
What is the City trying to hear?

. . . Spirit, appear!
. . . What is the destiny of the wounded City?
Those who listen can still hear its pulse,
the strong, seething life in its ancient roots. . . .[21]

This excerpt from a Rwandan song shows the contrast of life before and after:

Lament of Victims of Genocide

Suzanne Nyiranyamibwa

. . . Wild grass has hidden the county paths
The beautiful hills of yesteryear are covered in ruins
There where children frolicked and played
Are places where vultures now roam
The tears of orphans give you no relief from pain
Mothers have had their children ripped from their breasts
Too many widows trapped between life and death. . . .[22]

Today in western cultures, the singing about death, dirges, and destruction is more common in popular cultural songs and literary poems than in everyday religious rituals or worship. In general, there has been a separating of this subject from religious spheres, except for funeral contexts. Even in funerals, the genre of the dirge lament song for the particular person lost has been dramatically removed and replaced, sometimes, by a spoken eulogy. What has been lost in this trend? What is lost when we give up grieving expressions of our humanity, our loved one, and what we valued?

Now let us shift from laments of the dirge type to the other kind of lament—*prayer to the deity*. Just as dirges have typical features, so do lament prayers. Not every prayer is a lament, of course; some prayers extol God, or are meditations brought to God, for example. But the core of lament prayer is the twofold expression of suffering or need, and the plea to the deity for help.[23] Psalm 13 is an example of a lament prayer from the Hebrew Bible. Note the painfully honest questions, audacious but very common in lament prayer, and the imperative pleas.

> How long, O LORD?
> Will you forget me forever?
> How long will you hide your face from me?
> How long must I bear pain in my soul,
> and have sorrow in my heart all day long?
> How long shall my enemy be exalted over me?
>
> Consider and answer me, O LORD my God!
> Give light to my eyes, or I will
> sleep the sleep of death,
> and my enemy will say,
> "I have prevailed";
> my foes will rejoice because I am shaken.
>
> But I trusted in your steadfast love;
> my heart shall rejoice in your salvation.
> I will sing to the LORD,
> because he has dealt bountifully with me. (Ps 13:1-6)

The biblical psalms are the influential early paradigm for lament prayer among the Abrahamic faiths, though of course the traditions developed their own variations through authoritative collections, as well as local cultural and religious contexts. The exodus experience of the Hebrew slaves rescued from bondage (c. 1300 B.C.E.), when God saw their plight, heard their lament, and rescued them, was the historical raw material that established the psalmic "lament to praise" pattern. Not all laments move to an assurance of being heard, or to praise at all, as is the case in the psalm above. But this structure of appeal reflects a theology now found in Jewish, Christian, and Muslim lament prayers; it is also found in other world religions and spiritual traditions in which a deity is appealed to through prayer. Especially important in the biblical psalms are the lamenters' complaints about *injustice*, or about received mistreatment or oppression against oneself or against others, thus explaining their call for justice and help based on Torah ethics. We will return to look further at biblical lament psalms in a later chapter.

There were traditions of lament prayer before the biblical canon among ancient cultures and that continue in indigenous cultures today. Here are some examples of lament prayers and songs across cultures and religious traditions that express the human voice, often on behalf of a particular community, rendering a cry of lament for help to the supreme deity.

The Sun Dance ceremony, practiced by numerous tribes of the American Plains Indians, is a time of prayer and selfless ritual, a complex and meaningful community gathering and feast, the preparation and observance of which extends over numerous days. According to Lame Deer, Lakota holy man, it is a ritual that is very old and has evolved over time. He reflects on the event from his tradition's perspective, imagining its origin:

> Huddling in poor shelters in the darkness of winter, freezing and hungry, hibernating almost like animals, how joyfully, thankfully they must have greeted the life-giving sun, let it warm their frozen bodies as spring returned. I can imagine one of them on a sudden impulse getting up to dance for the sun, using his body like a prayer, and all the others joining him one by one. . . . I told you of *hanble-chia*, the vision quest, one man, alone by himself on an isolated hilltop, communicating with the mystery power. Well, the sun dance is *all* the people communicating with *all* the mystery powers. It is the *hanblechia* of the whole Sioux nation. The sun dance is the most misunderstood of all our rites. Many white men think of it as an initiation into manhood, or a way to prove one's courage. But this is

wrong. The sun dance is a prayer and a sacrifice. One does not take part in it voluntarily but as the result of a dream, or a vision.[24]

In the Sun Dance, with the community gathered round, men (and sometimes women) dance in the sun for days around a sacred tree, becoming thirsty from the heat and from the ritual blowing of an eaglebone whistle. There are accompanying songs, drumming, and lament prayers, also led by medicine men. The tree has sacrificed itself and is respected and regarded as having been wounded and killed for the community. The men have presented themselves for this ritual, having already undergone a painful piercing of their flesh (chest or back) by the embedding of a thorn or bone that is attached to a long strip of leather or thong, and then attached to the center tree. As they dance, their body weight eventually tears the thorn or bone free from their flesh. Women may have cuts of flesh on their arms. This ritual undertaking is a commitment to personal sacrifice and suffering and praying to the Great Spirit, sometimes with tears, for one's own help and strength, but also in intercession for one's people, for help and blessing, and for the larger good. People may find physical healing in the ritual. One sun dancer described by Lame Deer made his sacrifice with a prayer for peace in Vietnam. Lame Deer explains:

> The idea of enduring pain so that others may live should not strike you as strange. . . . The difference between the white man and us is this: You believe in the redeeming powers of suffering, if this suffering was done by somebody else, far way, two thousand years ago. We believe it is up to every one of us to help each other, even through the pain of our bodies. Pain to us is not "abstract," but very real. We do not lay this burden onto our god, nor do we want to miss being face to face with the spirit power. . . . we experience the sudden insight, come closest to the mind of the Great Spirit.[25]

Since the prayers and songs are sacred, the actual ceremony is not included here for listening, but an example of a prayer/song can be listened to on the CD selection.[26]

In these many examples, one sees something that holds human beings together in a kind of universal extended family—suffering or need, and a spiritual plea for help.

The prevalence of *questions* in laments is very common across cultures and spiritual traditions. In popular music that especially challenges social injustice, such questions can be pervasive and haunting, directed to humans as much as to God, while the prayer element may disappear, sometimes becoming only implicit, or questions may buttress a secular moral appeal. A 1983 song from the political context of the conflict in Northern Ireland by the rock group U2, lamented over and over again the continuing futility of violence and death by using the refrain "How long?!"

Sunday, Bloody Sunday

U2

. . . How long, how long must we sing this song?
. . . Sunday, bloody Sunday.[27]

"God, Where Were You?" ("Mana Wari Uri He?") is a song by Jean Paul Samputu of Rwanda about the unspeakable tragedy of genocide, and which gains its force from this repeating question.[28] In South Africa, a single question runs through the powerful and beloved freedom song "Senzeni Na" ("What have we done?")—that is, what have we done to deserve this treatment?!

Senzeni Na

Senzeni na senzeni na
Senzeni na senzeni na
Senzeni na senzeni na
Senzeni na kulomhlaba?

What have we done, what have we done?
What have we done, what have we done?
What have we done, what have we done?
What have we done in this country (world)?
Boers are dogs
Boers are dogs . . .

It's a sin to be Black
It's a sin to be Black . . .

It's a sin to be Black
It's a sin in this country (world).[29]

The doctor from Gaza who lost his daughters, mentioned at the opening of this book, voiced a similar agonizing question over and over again: "What have we done to them? What have we done to them!"

The use of even more stinging questions by some poets audaciously challenges God's absence from and abandonment of their people, as in this poem by a Bosnian Croat. Written just prior to the outbreak of war in Croatia and Bosnia in 1991, it is a kind of response to the biblical psalm in which the ancient Judeans lamented from Babylonian captivity:

croatian psalm 137

Borislav Arapović

while still trembling on the edge of time
and in the depth of space
we heard the throb of our name
and the flow of the atoms
of our genes—gehennas

already on euphrates
at the tower of babel
you lined us up
into first ranks

we planted a tree amid cindered rafters
and on its top we stuck
glagolitic writing
and we have been waiting with no response
for eons on end

are we really the ones you will use
to put out the flame of the bush?

where is your abode
why are you not among us too

since you are everywhere
and if you are also with us
why do we not see that we are not alone? [30]

Such sardonic anguish and near despair is reminiscent of the prophet Jeremiah in his laments to God at the time of the devastation of Jerusalem.

The above laments cannot help but imply ideological or theological beliefs and values of an individual, community, its culture or religion, and thus work to conserve and/or innovate such understandings or worldviews.

In the next chapter we turn to some of the significant lament traditions in the Bible that have been influential in many cultures of the world.

PART TWO

———⊗∞∞⊗———

Lament in the
Abrahamic Sacred Texts and
Contemporary Cultures

We turn now to the sacred texts of Judaism, Christianity, and Islam—the Tanak/Hebrew Bible, New Testament, and Qur'an—for an exploration of how lament forms appear there. We will include many contemporary popular cultural examples of poems or songs that share features with lament in the sacred texts.

CHAPTER THREE

The Grounding of Lament in the Hebrew Bible

The First Biblical Lament—from the Children, outside Eden

> Your brother's blood is crying out to me from the ground! (Gen 4:10b)

For those communities in cultures worldwide that adopt biblical tradition as a full or partial grounding for faith and life, the Exodus liberation narrative and the lament psalms in the Tanak/Hebrew Bible/Old Testament provide the primary theological paradigm for lament genres. Virtually all cultures have always had lament prayer and dirge forms, so when Judaism, Christianity, or Islam (all practicing a monotheistic theology of prayer) became rooted in various local cultures, there would have been an engagement over time between lament forms of the scriptures and a particular culture's existing lament forms. The result is not a slavish imitation of laments of the Bible, but the creative generation of laments by the peoples of local cultures, influenced by the sacred texts, yet developing distinctive expressions shaped by the needs and practices of their communities. The following is not a comprehensive study of the texts in the Bible and the Qur'an, but an illuminating of a representative number of sacred texts that participate in the practice of lament.

The first real lament to appear as the Hebrew Bible unfolds is the cry of the blood of Abel. God hears the cry and says to Cain, who took Abel's life,

> What have you done? Listen; your brother's blood is crying out to me from the ground!

Implicit in this lean story is that God had been pleased with Abel's ritual offering, but not so much with Cain's, for he does not appear to make the extra effort to bring anything from the "first fruits" of his crop, while Abel brings a choice animal sacrifice from the best of his flock. God's lack of regard for Cain's offering evokes a despondent, angry reaction in Cain, much like a child might respond to a displeased father. Perhaps there is a profound psychological insight here—that lack of acceptance or encouragement of a child's efforts (or perceived lack), or a child's being neglected or treated badly, may contribute to that child's insecurity and subsequent damaging behavior toward others, with negative repercussions also for him or her. Carrying unresolved psychological and emotional issues of sibling rivalry also might involve an "adult child's" later denial of such reality/need, or owning responsibility for ongoing destructive attitudes and actions. However, there are many dimensions to be learned from the story's wisdom, especially as it evokes the reader's or hearer's responses.

Though the storyteller depicts these brothers as being among the first humans, anachronistically they are expected to know the proper custom of bringing an offering to God, along with a glad, not grudging, attitude, trusting that if they give up the best, God will provide them with more. Before the tragic outcome, as God notices and addresses Cain's anger, God encourages him to do the good, and he will be lifted up, not downcast (and by implication—regarded well). Otherwise, God warns, sin will get the better of him, but Cain must master it. Yet, the story line suggests that Cain allows his anger and jealousy to overcome him and to drive his violent lashing out, resulting in Abel's demise and his own displacement. God asks him, "Where is your brother?" The eleventh-century Jewish commentator Rashi suggests that God is here giving Cain a chance to confess.[1] But Cain gives the now infamous reply of feigned innocence: "I do not know; am I my brother's keeper?" God tells him: "now you are cursed from the ground . . . it will no longer yield to you . . . you will be a fugitive and a wanderer on the earth" (Gen 4:9, 11-12).

Cain then utters a further lament: "My punishment is greater than I can bear! Today you have driven me away from the soil, and I shall be hidden from your face; I shall be a fugitive and a wanderer on the earth, and anyone who meets me may kill me." (Gen. 4:13-14) Cain attributes the cause of punishment to God, yet the story suggests that this outcome for him actually comes as a consequence of his own actions. The outcome is a joint moral response from the natural and human worlds, because he has gone down the path of damaging relationships with both, which will have future repercussions. While the story contains truths, it is also troubling, for it suggests a universal problem of the suffering of both the victim and the punished victimizer. Cain leaves, losing perhaps what he wanted most—God's positive regard—and settles further east of Eden in the land of Nod ("wandering"), yet carrying God's promise to protect his life. This is not to be underestimated. Cain retains a relationship with God; God does not forsake him.

Oddly enough, the storyteller didn't record a direct discourse of the cry or lament of Abel; only figuratively is his blood described as crying out. Only God hears and attends to that lament. This too is profoundly suggestive—this is a God whose compassion goes out to the victim, but who does not neglect the feelings and the future of the wrongdoer either. It is suggestive, as well, for so often the vulnerable victims (the poor, the powerless) are abused secretly, and may suffer and then die alone with their voices unheard in the larger community or within society's structures. But God knows. In other places, the Bible records this rhetorical feature of innocent blood that is shed and that cries out for justice and vindication (for example, Job 16:18), suggesting the social idea and/or custom (joined with the sacred/deity) of what has been called "blood vengeance" in some ancient cultures, including parts of the Bible (cf.

Num 35:19-33), where the redeemer of blood (*goel*) is expected to exact justice by punishing the perpetrator. For instance, God says to Noah:

> For your own lifeblood I will surely require a reckoning: from every animal I will require it and from human beings, each one for the blood of another, I will require a reckoning for human life. Whoever sheds the blood of a human, by a human shall that person's blood be shed; for in his own image God made humankind. (Gen 9:5-6)

Ironically, there is no reckoning in the text required of God, who has wiped out humankind with the flood. In the story of Cain and Abel, God knows and pays attention to the wronged individual; however, again significantly, God does not take the life of Cain for taking the life of Abel, but shows Cain mercy. This early story in the Bible overturns a traditional custom of blood vengeance; God also prevents the killing of Cain by others who might seek retribution.[2] God's created order exacts a justice by allowing the consequences of Cain's actions—alienation from the land and from humans—to banish Cain. Yet, we might ask, where was God's justice for Abel to prevent his death? As in life, there is a troubling mixture of both comforting hope and a question about this God. If God cares and loves, why did God not have regard for both Cain and Abel unconditionally, and why did God not intervene to rescue Abel? Perhaps God did love Cain, but Cain perceived God's correcting him as lack of love and acceptance—a pivotal moment also in parent-child relations.

Post-biblical popular Jewish retellings of the story (and interpretations and homilies based on them, called the *aggadah*) fill in some of the gaps in the biblical text. A few of these implicitly take issue with God by defending Cain, whose jealousy seemed to have been provoked by God's favoritism of Abel. For example, in one *aggadic* rendition Cain says:

> Am I my brother's keeper? Thou art He who holdest watch over all creatures ["keeper" in Hebrew can also be translated "one who guards" or "watches over"], and yet Thou demandest account of

me! True, I slew him, but Thou didst create the evil inclination in me. Thou guardest all things; why, then, didst Thou permit me to slay him? Thou didst Thyself slay him, for hadst Thou looked with a favorable countenance toward my offering as toward his, I had had no reason for envying him, and I had not slain him.[3]

In any event, the narrative suggests that the twofold curse of the ground and a life of hardship, stemming also from the parents' disobedience in the Garden of Eden story, both continue in the lives of the children. An ancient story suggests the common human experience of a dysfunctional family pattern that continues to produce suffering from generation to generation, unless the cycle is broken. In the Qur'an, Cain and Abel are referenced not by name but as "Adam's two sons" (in Surat al-Ma'ida/The Feast 5:27-31), where the biblical account is assumed, but an additional conversation between the brothers is given. Cain threatens to kill Abel, but Abel says, "If you raise your hand to kill me, I will not raise mine to kill you." He wishes further that Cain will be punished for his sin. Cain still kills Abel, but the text says that he becomes remorseful upon burying him.[4] In secular literature, Ricardo Quinones's book, *The Changes of Cain* traces how western classics through the centuries have retold this seminal story in ever more modern garb.[5]

Laments for Loss of Paradise

While the cry of Abel's blood is the first actual lament in the Bible's unfolding, the prior story of the Garden of Eden provides plenty of occasion for lament. Again, the post-biblical Jewish aggadot contain more detailed accounts about Adam and Eve in Eden, depicting a movement from a great joyous celebration of creation on the first Sabbath, to suffering and sadness, weeping and lament over losses in Eden. For example, in the aggadot, Lilith is revealed as being Adam's "first wife," given to him by God and also created from the ground. She left him when she insisted on equality and, presumably, didn't get it. She fled, preferring a severe punishment and a negative reputation rather than to endure staying with him. Adam lamented to God about her departure.[6]

There are numerous other laments among the aggadot on the Eden story; for example, before the disobedience, Adam prays a lament to God that plants might grow to provide for their food. The disobedience and consequences produce lamentable suffering, not only for the serpent, and Adam and Eve, but also for the earth (cursed, along with the serpent).[7] For example, the aggadah says,

> The earth also had to suffer a tenfold punishment: independent before, she was hereafter to wait to be watered by the rain from above; sometimes the fruits of the earth fail; the grain she brings forth is stricken with blasting and mildew; she must produce all sorts of noxious vermin . . . much is sown in the earth, but little is harvested. . . . When the serpent seduced Adam and Eve, and exposed their nakedness, they wept bitterly, and with them wept the heavens, and the sun and the stars, and all created beings and things up to the throne of God. The very angels and celestial beings were grieved by the transgression of Adam.[8]

Note the feature of earth and cosmos lamenting as persons. Here we have the traditional spiritual worldview noted earlier, a disharmony and breaking of the links between them and the source of energy, life, and harmony—God. Such wholesale lament, however, did not include a genuine "confessional" lament from Adam and Eve in Eden, according to the aggadah. Had it been offered, God then would have "permitted them to remain in Paradise, if only they had been penitent." When God commanded the angels to expel Adam and Eve from Eden, "they began to weep and supplicate bitterly, and the angels took pity upon them and left the Divine command unfulfilled, until they could petition [lament to] God to mitigate His severe verdict." Adam wept again and lamented, asking at least to take spices from Eden to use in his prayer offerings, and this he was granted. Once outside of paradise, Adam and Eve built a hut and sat mourning and lamenting for seven days. When they had no luck finding food, Adam decided they should do penance, with him standing in the river Jordan, and Eve in the Tigris, both up to their necks(!) while Adam also fasted. He suggested to Eve not to lament to God as their lips were unclean. Upon their first recognition of the sun going down, they wept and lamented again, believing that the world was coming to an end because of them. The aggadic tradition suggests that their many lament prayers were finally answered by God, who sent the angel Raziel to teach Adam wisdom. Upon the death of Adam, and later Eve, angels were sent to show the survivors how to bury their loved ones until the general resurrection.[9]

As if this suffering in the Genesis stories of early humans were not enough, there is the tendency through the centuries to blame Eve for (the traditional view of) "the fall of man," and thus to blame all womankind. Some early Jewish, and many more Christian interpreters, blame Eve, though the Qur'an does not in its rendering of the story. Those interpretations blaming Eve, and the associated restrictive practices against women in some cultures, regardless of claimed religious principles, have surely created much suffering and the occasion for lament by countless women worldwide, whose social and spiritual statuses have been and continue to be denigrated. Ironically, while the sacred texts (the Hebrew Bible, the New Testament, and the Qur'an) all created some significant gains for women in their times, egalitarian treatment and women's civil rights made gains only after the Enlightenment and within constitutional democracies, through the opening up of more opportunities to women, especially toward the end of the twentieth century. Yet modern cultures also often carry exploitative sexual views toward women that many view as denigrating.[10]

The Paradigm: Exodus Lament

> Out of slavery, their cry for help rose up to God.
> (Exod 2:23)

As we have seen, forms of lament appear across cultures and in sacred texts, expressing shared experiences of suffering, need, prayer pleas, and appeals for remedying injustice. But the narrative of the liberation experience of the Hebrew slaves in the book of Exodus forms the paradigm for suffering and rescue, for lament and transformed experience to praise, not only for Hebrew and later Israelite and Jewish traditions. Christian and Muslim sacred texts and their interpretive histories also recognize the importance of the exodus experience and the characterization of a God who is compassionate and who intervenes against injustice to answer cries of suffering.[11]

In his classic study *The Prophetic Imagination*, Walter Brueggemann suggested that the story of Moses and the Hebrews in Egypt marked a

> radical break from both the religion of static triumphalism and the politics of oppression and exploitation. . . . The mythic claims of the empire are ended by the disclosure of *the alternative religion of the freedom of God* . . . [and] *a politics of justice and compassion* . . . the emergence of a new social community in history.[12]

By both "criticizing" the old arrangement and by grieving their suffering, Moses and the people find "energizing" through God's power and freedom to act on their own behalf. Says Brueggemann

> The real criticism begins in the capacity to grieve because that is the most visceral announcement that things are not right. Only in the empire are we pressed and urged and invited to pretend that things are all right . . . The Exodus is the primal scream that permits the beginning of history. The verb "cry out" . . . also functions for the official filing of a legal complaint . . . Israel does not voice resignation but instead it expresses a militant sense of being wronged . . . The life of freedom and justice comes when they risk the freedom of the free God against the regime . . . Bringing hurt to public expression is an important first step in the dismantling criticism that permits a new reality, theological and social, to emerge.[13]

The exodus story has spoken to peoples around the world and infused modern "liberation theologies," developed among indigenous peoples and priests in Latin America and by African American, African, and Asian leaders, but their own stories have also shed new light upon the exodus story. Exodus has been a freedom story of hope for many who are oppressed around the world.[14] All this suggests that liberation is a partisan enterprise—this God is (necessarily) on the side of oppressed, innocent sufferers, and has a "preferential option for the poor." Yet, there is a danger, too often not stated, that this partisan care does not always expand into liberation and care for all peoples of the world together, in principle. The positive potential of what God can do, and what the world can become, can be lost in partisanship, disbursing into eddies and pockets of "us" and "them," with separate claims staked out, perhaps once again at the other's expense. Indeed, the danger of joining the liberation narrative to a "conquest of land" ideology, sanctioned by God, is being critiqued by commentators and readers who are themselves colonized people in the world, and thus sympathetic to the Canaanites in the Bible. Those of us from powerful nations with a history of such colonizing must take care in our assumptions, standing instead with our struggling heritage of freedom for all.[15]

We do not have a "lament lyric" in the liberation story of Exodus (though later lyrics in the Psalms and Prophets allude to the liberation experience), but a narrative that summarizes the oppression of the slaves. Certainly, though, one can assume that the retelling of the story was likely in "oral poetic" form, customary to traditional cultures: They "made their lives bitter with hard service in mortar and brick and in every kind of field labor. They were ruthless in all the tasks that they imposed on them" (Exod 1:14). When Pharaoh imposes a policy of genocide, of killing male babies, the faithful Hebrew midwives undertake a quiet protest of resistance. Their foiling of Pharaoh's plan, in cooperation with Miriam, Moses' sister, and in response to their people's lament and agony, allows God to make inroads against Pharaoh's power, eventually dismantling it.[16]

The summary text often cited is Exodus 2:23-25, prior to Moses' call:

> After a long time the king of Egypt died. The Israelites groaned under their slavery, and cried out [zā'aq]. Out of the slavery their cry for help rose up to God. God heard their groaning, and God remembered his covenant with Abraham, Isaac, and Jacob. God looked upon the Israelites, and God took notice of them.

And, God says,

> I have observed the misery of my people who are in Egypt; I have heard their cry [tse'aqah] on account of their taskmasters. Indeed,

I know their sufferings, and I have come down to deliver them from the Egyptians, and to bring them up out of that land to a good and broad land, a land flowing with milk and honey, to the country of the Canaanites, the Hittites, the Amorites, the Perizzites, the Hivites, and the Jebusites. The cry [*tse'aqah*] of the Israelites has now come to me; I have also seen how the Egyptians oppress them. (Exod 3:7-9)

The verb (and noun) forms of the Hebrew root words, *tsa'aq* and *za'aq*, are the primary signals for lament in Exodus. Patrick Miller's study suggests those terms, along with *qara'* (to "call upon" or "cry out"), *shivva'* (to "cry out"), and *siakh* (to "complain"), all usually refer to persons lamenting who are poor, weak, oppressed, victimized, or innocent.[17] Those who lament in the Psalms, particularly, use these terms, and the character Job is noted for his use of the last term. The term to "pray" (*hitpallel*; "prayer": *tefillah*) is more general and may include a lament or other types of prayer to God. Similarly the general term *'atar* connotes "entreaty," and may mean intercession on another's behalf. Even simple verbs such as to "say," "speak," "seek," "ask," or "inquire" can connote conversation with God that is informal prayer, a bringing of something to God's attention for consideration.[18] A third key term, *khanan*, suggests to "make supplication" or "plea" for God's mercy, favor, grace, or kindness. It may be combined with a lament for rescue to the One who is merciful.[19]

The unfolding imposition of plagues against Egypt by God and Moses is intended to exert pressure on the (new) pharaoh, in effect, through a reversal of hardship or suffering—turning the tables against him and his people. During the course of the plagues, Pharaoh asks Moses to make entreaty (*'atar*) to YHWH to stop the plagues. Ironically, Moses does, but the alleviation of hardship does not then cause Pharaoh to see the light and turn to YHWH or to free the Hebrews. His interests are, first, for his political state and his own power, stubbornly adhered to even when his policy continues to severely hurt his own people, now crying out in lament. In Exodus 12:30, as a result of the final plague of the deaths of his own people's firstborn, "there was a loud cry (*tse'aqah*) in Egypt." (Here again is an ideology embedded in the Scripture that is troubling, in which God is portrayed as purposefully allowing the deaths of innocent children as a tool to effect liberation).[20] At one point, Pharaoh breaks down and tells the Hebrews to leave, but in the end, he will not relinquish his final pursuit of them, to his own demise. (It appears that ill-conceived, unethical policy and the poor exercise of judgment are not simply characteristics of present-day political leaders.) At the climactic moment when the Hebrews are about to escape, Moses says to them: "Don't be afraid, stand firm, and see the deliverance that the Lord will accomplish for you today; for the Egyptians whom you see today you shall never see again. The Lord will fight for you, and you have only to keep still." Then the Lord said to Moses (who was perhaps lamenting their dire straits), "Why do you cry out [*tsa'aq*] to me? Tell the Israelites to go forward" (Exod 14:13-15). Apparently, there is a time to lament and a time to get moving! Only after their miraculous protection and the defeat of Pharaoh's army do the Hebrews sing a song of praise to God, to YHWH who has saved them:

> I will sing to the LORD!
>> for he has triumphed gloriously;
>>> horse and rider he has thrown into the sea.
> The LORD is my strength and my might,
> and he has become my salvation;
> this is my God, and I will praise him,
> my father's God, and I will exalt him. . . . (Exod 15:1b-2)

Echos of Exodus

The Jewish Passover Seder ritual, instituted in ancient times, commemorates the exodus liberation by way of the Haggadah (retelling) and has been celebrated in Jewish homes through the generations unto today. Even the sad fate of the Egyptians in this story is attended to in some versions of the ritual through sorrow expressed (lament) for the loss of Egyptian lives, thus tempering the celebration of the Hebrews' escape to freedom.[21]

As is well known, the Exodus freedom story inspired black slaves in America. African-American theologian James Cone opens his book

The Spirituals and the Blues by saying, "The power of song in the struggle for black survival—that is what the spirituals and the blues are about," and ". . . the spirituals and the blues were a way of life, an artistic affirmation of the meaningfulness of black existence . . . I, therefore, write about the spirituals and the blues, because *I am the blues* and *my life is a spiritual.* Without them, I cannot be."[22] As Melva W. Costen describes, "Slaves understood clearly that the Holy Spirit is free to move at will and cannot be manipulated. Singing, whether as prayer or as a response to prayers and other elements of worship, helped create a mood of freedom, an openness to quicken an awareness of God's presence, and for the hearing and receiving of God's grace."[23] Harriet Tubman, who led many slaves to freedom along the dangerous "underground railroad," was called the "Moses" of her people. (It is interesting that she was not called the "Miriam" of her people; gender was less important than God's call to a primary leadership role.) An excerpt of the spiritual "Go Down, Moses" sung by Paul Robeson, may be listened to through a link on this book's website.

Go Down, Moses

When Israel was in Egypt's land
Let my people go
Oppressed so hard they could not stand
Let my people go

Go down Moses
Way down in Egypt land
Tell old Pharaoh
"Let my people go"

"Thus spoke the Lord" bold Moses said
"Let my people go
If not I'll smite your first born dead"
Let my people go

"No more in bondage shall they toil"
Let my people go
"Let them come out with Egypt's spoil"
Let my people go.[24]

An additional lament of Moses in the Bible should be mentioned here, to show his character as a lamenter. It comes from Numbers 11, subsequent to God's rescue of the Hebrews, when they are moving through the desert and facing new hardships.

Now when the people complained in the hearing of the LORD about their misfortunes, the LORD heard it and his anger was kindled. Then the fire of the LORD burned against them, and consumed some outlying parts of the camp. But the people cried out to Moses; and Moses prayed to the LORD, and the fire abated. . . . The rabble among them had a strong craving; and the Israelites also wept again, and said, "If only we had meat to eat! We remember the fish we used to eat in Egypt for nothing, the cucumbers, the melons, the leeks, the onions, and the garlic; but now our strength is dried up, and there is nothing at all but this manna to look at. . . ." Moses heard the people weeping throughout their families, all at the entrances of their tents. Then the LORD became very angry, and Moses was displeased. So Moses said to the LORD, "Why have you treated your servant so badly? Why have I not found favor in your sight, that you lay the burden of all this people on me? Did I conceive all this people? Did I give birth to them, that you should say to me, 'Carry them in your bosom, as a nurse carries a sucking child,' to the land that you promised on oath to their ancestors? Where am I to get meat to give to all this people? For they come weeping to me and say, 'Give us meat to eat!' I am not able to carry all this people alone, for they are too heavy for me. If this is the way you are going to treat me, put me to death at once—if I have found favor in your sight—and do not let me see my misery."

So the LORD said to Moses, "Gather for me seventy of the elders of Israel, whom you know to be the elders of the people and officers over them; bring them to the tent of meeting, and have them take their place there with you. I will come down and talk with you there; and I will take some of the spirit that is on you and put it on them; and they shall bear the burden of the people along with you so that you will not bear it all by yourself. And say to the people: Consecrate yourselves for tomorrow, and you shall eat meat; for you have wailed in the hearing of the LORD, saying, 'If only we had meat to eat! Surely it was better for us in Egypt.' Therefore the LORD will give you meat, and you shall eat. You shall eat not only one day, or two days, or five days, or ten days, or twenty days, but for a whole month—until it comes out of your nostrils and becomes loathsome to you—because you have rejected the LORD who is among you, and have wailed before him, saying, 'Why did we ever leave Egypt?'" But Moses said, "The people I am with number six hundred thousand on foot; and you say, 'I will give them meat, that they may eat for a whole month'! Are there enough flocks and herds to slaughter for them? Are there enough fish in the sea to catch for them?" The LORD said to Moses, "Is the LORD's power limited? Now you shall see whether my word will come true for you or not. . . ." Then a wind went out from the LORD, and it brought quails from the sea and let them fall beside the camp, about a day's journey on this side and a day's journey on the other side, all around the camp, about two cubits deep on the ground. (Num 11:1-2, 4-6, 10-23, 31)

While Moses appears rather strident here, his sister Miriam, identified also as a prophet in Exodus 15:20 (and suggested in Micah 6:4), has her own tough side. To be fair, the circumstances of crisis must have called for it, just as today's prophetic figures are some of the toughest people in the world. Some rabbinic traditions suggest that Miriam's contributions as a prophet include her dreams or visions from God, guiding her to rescue the infant Moses. A recent study suggests that her role as a singer (Exod 15) is congruent with prophetic activity, as biblical prophets sang or rhythmically chanted their messages.[25]

In Numbers 12:1-16, Miriam and Aaron challenge Moses with a complaint and a lament aired before God. God's response favors Moses over their complaint, yet here we see again the Hebraic tradition's inclusion of lament; it is not out of bounds in the wrangling of faith. Some feminists and womanists suggest that the story's patriarchal perspective, more than its "religious" perspective, is what renders Miriam in the wrong, rather than Moses, whose actions are challenged.[26] In this text, God is presented as an offended patriarch whose judgment is challenged by a woman, who is then punished. Interestingly, the views of "the people" are not given, but they do not move on in their journey until Miriam is restored to them.

The acceptance of such dissenting lament by the faithful before God, of such candor and truth-telling, as humans see it, as being without regard for the consequences, has been more characteristic of the Jewish Tanakh than of Christian Scriptures or the Qur'an. Yet all three traditions stress the importance of lament prayer, as supplication or plea to God, as will be seen. Perhaps it is not too much of an oversimplification to suggest that Jewish tradition saw no contradiction between faithfulness to God and lament that is complaint or protest about hardships, injustice, and even God's role. Lament aimed to change unacceptable circumstances through God's agency; this was the lesson of the exodus experience. As the above text also suggests, apart from gender issues, the human lamenter may push a little too far into God's domain, and the deity pushes back to draw a line between the divine and the human. This we will see shortly in the example of Job. Yet overall, the Hebrew Bible affirms the legitimacy of such lament simply by the long heritage of including it.

On the other hand, Christian and Muslim traditions, especially after their early periods, have leaned toward understanding faith, when in severely difficult situations, as implying the acceptance of God's will, or as submission to Allah, respectively, more than in lament as protest. There is revealed wisdom in this, too. And in the Hebrew Bible, a particular strand of the wisdom tradition follows more along this approach, a counter to the lament tradition, that by doing good and exercising trusting patience—while "fearing [revering] God"—the "righteous" will be taken care of by God and rewarded. In Christianity, exceptions to mere acceptance/submission have been those black and ethnic Christians around the globe who, out of their slavery or suffering, joined with the Jewish approach to lament and made bold calls for change. This suggests that a religious tradition's stance about lament could be related to the comfort zone of its own "social location."

In both Anglo-European Christian traditions and Muslim traditions, is there not perhaps an unresolved tension about simply accepting life's suffering and injustices, whether one's own or that of other people? After all, the origins of Christianity and Islam might be looked upon as God's answering the laments of those suffering and oppressed in the particular sociohistorical cultures in which these religions emerged. Perhaps Christianity and Islam came to emphasize the simple acceptance of the all-sufficient character of the deity's way of taking care of things, particularly where its cultures gained power. And Judaism, even with its legacy of prophetic lament and social justice for all, may neglect these when preoccupied as a people in survival mode. Those representing the three Abrahamic faiths may neglect God's compassionate involvement to transform history in order to reach *all* suffering humanity, including the alien, the orphan, the widow, and the oppressed. When we participate in any actions or attitudes that neglect or hurt others, rather than show such justice and compassion, we have not only departed from being true to our traditions, but most importantly, from the One to whom we must answer.

"Texts of Terror"

> Tamar put ashes on her head, and tore the long robe
> that she was wearing; she put her hand on her head, and
> went away, crying aloud as she went. (2 Sam 13:19)

Any discussion of lament in the Hebrew Bible should recollect a number of female characters in narratives whom Phyllis Trible illuminated, in her book *Texts of Terror*, as having been especially victimized, about whom God was not recorded as having said anything, and thus allowing for the misogyny, or hatred of women, evident in parts of the Bible.[27] The neglect of their stories in commentaries and in faith communities has had a detrimental effect on the treatment of women throughout history. The biblical women addressed by Trible included Hagar, the Egyptian slave (Gen 16, 21); Tamar, who was raped (2 Sam 13); Jephthah's daughter, who was sacrificed (Judg 11); and the unnamed concubine who was brutally killed (Judg 19). And there are others. These stories, and the women by their presence and brutalized bodies, serve in a sense as voiceless laments.[28] More recently, feminist and womanist interpreters are drawing attention to the misogynist language in parts of the prophetic literature that personify Jerusalem (representative of the people and leaders) as an unfaithful wife or disobedient daughter to be brutally punished by God.[29] Such interpreters, for some, ironically by their very critique, transform these texts into a hope for those still victimized today in cultures that would unfortunately condone abuse of women—that women's experiences will be brought to light and they will be helped. The interpreters also cast light on the complicated issue of the Scripture, or any sacred text or its interpretation, that mingles patriarchal or dominant-class abuse, or limitation of women's or human rights with God's will. This is certainly not to say that patriarchal, traditional cultures or religions are only bad or abusive of women; that would be an unfair oversimplification.

———— ∝◊∞ ————

CHAPTER FOUR

Lament as Prayerful Plea in the Abrahamic Sacred Texts

A survey of the scriptures of the three Abrahamic faiths reveals that the preponderance of lament elements in all three takes the form of *lament prayer* or *appeal to the deity for help*. In the New Testament, a few individuals also appeal to Jesus as Messiah for help.

The Hebrew Psalms: Suffering and Complaints of Injustice

> Give ear to my words, O LORD; give heed to my sighing.
> Listen to the sound of my cry. (Ps 5:1)

The psalms in the Hebrew Bible carry forward the paradigm of lament from Exodus, offering up many expressions of lament as prayerful plea. Commentators differ on how many psalms to designate as laments in the psalter—some as few as one-third. My count is that nearly half the psalms (73 of 150) include the essential lament element—the plea to God for help. At times, other features or another genre of a psalm may overshadow the plea. The makeup of the psalter suggests that there was an intentional balance between lament and praise when the canon was crystallized. An additional thirty non lament psalms still include a reference to former laments that God has answered, moving the representation of lament prayer to 103 out of 150 songs. The psalms often, but not always, contain the movement from lament to praise (about 29 of 73 above), like the pattern seen in the resolution of the Exodus liberation story from lament to praise in Exodus 15.

Readers are encouraged to read the following psalms that contain lament and to consult the commentaries[1] for a full analysis of the poems (the psalms marked with an asterisk are confessional in nature): Psalms 3, 4, 5, 6, 7, 9, 10, 12, 13, 16, 17, 22, 25*, 26, 27, 28, 31, 32*, 35, 36, 38*, 39*, 40, 41*, 42, 43, 44, 51*, 54, 55, 56, 57, 58, 59, 60, 61, 62, 63, 64, 69*, 70, 71, 72, 74, 77, 79, 80, 82, 83, 85*, 86, 88, 89, 90*, 94, 102, 106*, 108, 109, 119, 120, 123, 125, 126, 129, 130*, 137, 139, 140, 141, 142, 143, and 144.

Many commentators identify the following typical parts of biblical lament prayer songs, based on the psalms. We have begun to see how some of these elements also naturally appear across poems and songs of other religious traditions and cultures. Not all of these occur in every biblical lament, or in this order:

1) address to the deity (second person speech);
2) complaint or description of distress, often with questions (to or against the deity, about one's enemies, and/or about one's suffering);
3) expression of trust in the deity and/or remembrance of past saving actions;
4) petition/plea to the deity (using imperative verbs);

---

5) assurance of being heard;
6) vow of praise;
7) praise of the deity.

It is a profound matter that the reason most often mentioned for a person's lament in the biblical psalms is that they are being mistreated or oppressed by an enemy or adversary, though sometimes by a friend. Thus there is a *preoccupation with justice issues* in lament psalms. This raises questions about the possible vulnerable social location of the composers/singers. Here again is Psalm 13, quoted earlier, where we already noted the questions typical of the complaint of a lament prayer. The elements above are now indicated, including distress about "my enemy."

How long, O LORD?	[1 & 2]
Will you forget me forever?	[1 & 2]
How long will you hide your face from me?	[1 & 2][2]
How long must I bear pain in my soul,	
and have sorrow in my heart all day long?	[1 & 2]
How long shall my enemy be exalted over me?	[1 & 2]
Consider and answer me, O LORD my God!	[1 & 4]
Give light to my eyes, or I will	
sleep the sleep of death,	[4 & 2]
and my enemy will say,	
"I have prevailed";	[2]
my foes will rejoice because I am shaken.	[2]
———————	
But I trusted in your steadfast love;	[3]
my heart shall rejoice in your salvation.	[6 & 7]
I will sing to the LORD,	[6 & 7]
because he has dealt bountifully with me.	[5]

The line added in the middle of the psalm suggests the transition from lament to praise and intervention by God, help for the lamenter, indicated by a shift in verb tense from imperative plea for help to past or completed action (perfect tense in Hebrew), effected by God. Not every lament has this movement. As mentioned, some lamenters are left hanging, waiting for a response or intervention. Indeed, some 44 of the 73 lament psalms remain, within the text, unanswered or waiting for help, suggestive of the hard realities of life, in which the faithful wait for God's intervention—sometimes a long time coming. It is possible that some of the self-standing praise and thanksgiving psalms are the lament singers' responses to God's intervention for which they had prayed. Some commentators have suggested that perhaps a prophet intoned a comfort lyric ("salvation oracle") in response to the lamenter.[3] More recent commentators are exploring occasional dialogues of sometimes disagreeing perspectives within the psalms—for example, a didactic voice defending God's character might answer a lamenter complaining of God's failure to help.[4] Of course, once originated, songs would have been sung and re-sung, innovated and revised along the way to meet the needs of the community members over many generations.

Here is an example of a lament left unanswered in the text, Psalm 42:1-11:

> *To the leader. A Maskil of the Korahites*
> As a deer longs for flowing streams,
>   so my soul longs for you, O God.
> My soul thirsts for God, for the living God.
> When shall I come and behold the face of God?
> My tears have been my food day and night,
>   while people say to me continually, "Where is your God?"
> These things I remember, as I pour out my soul:
> how I went with the throng, and led them
>   in procession to the house of God,
> with glad shouts and songs of thanksgiving,
>   a multitude keeping festival.
> Why are you cast down, O my soul,
>   and why are you disquieted within me?
> Hope in God; for I shall again praise him, my help and my God.
> My soul is cast down within me;
> therefore I remember you
> from the land of Jordan and of Hermon, from Mount Mizar.
> Deep calls to deep at the thunder of your cataracts;
>   all your waves and your billows have gone over me.
> By day the LORD commands his steadfast love,
> and at night his song is with me, a prayer to the God of my life.
> I say to God, my rock, "Why have you forgotten me?

Why must I walk about mournfully because the enemy
     oppresses me?"
As with a deadly wound in my body, my adversaries taunt me,
while they say to me continually, "Where is your God?"
Why are you cast down, O my soul,
and why are you disquieted within me?
Hope in God; for I shall again praise him,
my help and my God.

While no divine answer or intervention is suggested, the lamenter ends on a positive note of confident hope that God will rescue, and he or she will then offer praise for divine help. This feature of praise in anticipation of help, in the midst of suffering, is a noted feature of the psalms and the singers' faith. We will see this feature again in African-American spirituals, gospel songs, and the blues, when people sang praises in the midst of hardship to lift their spirits.

The elements and metaphors of the biblical lament psalms are poetically compelling,[5] yet not so overly detailed or culture-bound that they cannot approach the experience of most individuals who are suffering (in antiquity or today), for example, from persecution, fear, illness, weakness, lack of guidance, or the shame of sin. Here are some of the compelling lyrics of *the plea*, in imperative tense, of biblical lament psalms:

I cry aloud to the LORD, and he answers from his holy hill . . .
Rise up, O LORD! Deliver me, O my God! (Ps 3:4, 7a)

Give ear to my words, O LORD; give heed to my sighing.
Listen to the sound of my cry . . . in the morning,
I plead my case to you, and watch. (Ps 5:1-2a, 3b)

Turn, O LORD, save my life;
deliver me for the sake of your steadfast love. . . .
I am weary with my moaning;
every night I flood my bed with tears;
I drench my couch with my weeping,
My eyes waste away because of my grief. . . . (Ps 6:4, 6-7a)

O Lord my God, in you I take refuge;
save me from all my pursuers, and deliver me,
or like a lion they will tear me apart. . . . (Ps 7:1-2a)

Be gracious to me, O Lord.
See what I suffer from those who hate me;
you are the one who lifts me up
from the gates of death,
so that I may recount all your praises . . .
Rise up, O Lord! Do not let mortals prevail;
let the nations be judged before you.
Put them in fear, O Lord;
let the nations know that they are only human.
        (Ps 9:13-14a, 19-20)

Why, O Lord, do you stand far off?
Why do you hide yourself in times of trouble?
In arrogance the wicked persecute the poor—
let them be caught in the schemes
they have devised. . . .
O Lord, you will hear the desire of the meek;
you will strengthen their heart,
you will incline your ear
to do justice for the orphan and the oppressed,
so that those from earth may strike terror no more.
        (Ps 10:1-2, 17-18)

Help, O Lord, for there is no longer anyone who is godly;
the faithful have disappeared from humankind.
They utter lies to each other;
with flattering lips and a double heart they speak. . . .

    "Because the poor are despoiled,
    because the needy groan,
    I will now rise up," says the Lord;
    "I will place them in the safety for which they long."
        (Ps 12:1-2, 5)

In addition, a psalm can be a communal lament offered for "our" suffering and appealing to God for help.[6] Psalm 74 is an example, also unanswered:

A Maskil of Asaph
O God, why do you cast us off forever?
Why does your anger smoke against the sheep of your pasture?
Remember your congregation, which you acquired long ago,
which you redeemed to be the tribe of your heritage.
Remember Mount Zion, where you came to dwell.
Direct your steps to the perpetual ruins;
the enemy has destroyed everything in the sanctuary.
Your foes have roared within your holy place;
they set up their emblems there.
At the upper entrance they hacked the wooden trellis with axes.
And then, with hatchets and hammers,
they smashed all its carved work.
They set your sanctuary on fire;
they desecrated the dwelling place of your name,
bringing it to the ground.
They said to themselves, "We will utterly subdue them";
they burned all the meeting places of God in the land.
We do not see our emblems; there is no longer any prophet,
and there is no one among us who knows how long.
How long, O God, is the foe to scoff?
Is the enemy to revile your name forever?
Why do you hold back your hand;
why do you keep your hand in your bosom?
Yet God my King is from of old, working salvation in the earth.
You divided the sea by your might;
you broke the heads of the dragons in the waters.
You crushed the heads of Leviathan;
you gave him as food for the creatures of the wilderness.
You cut openings for springs and torrents;
you dried up ever-flowing streams.
Yours is the day, yours also the night;

you established the luminaries and the sun.
You have fixed all the bounds of the earth;
you made summer and winter.
Remember this, O LORD, how the enemy scoffs,
and an impious people reviles your name.
Do not deliver the soul of your dove to the wild animals;
do not forget the life of your poor forever.
Have regard for your covenant,
for the dark places of the land are full of the haunts of violence.
Do not let the downtrodden be put to shame;
let the poor and needy praise your name.
Rise up, O God, plead your cause;
remember how the impious scoff at you all day long.
Do not forget the clamor of your foes,
the uproar of your adversaries that goes up continually.

A few laments among the psalms concern suffering from illness—for example, Psalms 6, 32, 38, 41, and 102. In all of these, the lamenter appears to attribute the suffering to his or her sinfulness, an ideology present in some parts of the Hebrew Bible. One wonders why there are no laments for illness among the psalms that do not interpret the cause of illness in this way. Of course, the immensely long book of Job covers plenty of ground debating these views, and appears to side with the latter.

Only ten lament psalms of the 150 appear to be confessional, seeking God's forgiveness for sin, though certainly ancient Israel had regular sacrificial rituals for atonement along with its confessional psalms. An example is Psalm 41:

To the leader. A Psalm of David
Happy are those who consider the poor;
the LORD delivers them in the day of trouble.
The LORD protects them and keeps them alive;
they are called happy in the land.
You do not give them up to the will of their enemies.
The LORD sustains them on their sickbed;
in their illness you heal all their infirmities.

As for me, I said, "O LORD, be gracious to me;
heal me, for I have sinned against you."
My enemies wonder in malice when I will die, and my name
    perish.
And when they come to see me, they utter empty words,
while their hearts gather mischief; when they go out, they tell it
    abroad.
All who hate me whisper together about me; they imagine the
    worst for me.
They think that a deadly thing has fastened on me,
that I will not rise again from where I lie.
Even my bosom friend in whom I trusted, who ate of my bread,
has lifted the heel against me.
But you, O LORD, be gracious to me,
and raise me up, that I may repay them.
By this I know that you are pleased with me;
because my enemy has not triumphed over me.
But you have upheld me because of my integrity,
and set me in your presence forever.
Blessed be the LORD, the God of Israel,
from everlasting to everlasting. Amen and Amen.

It should be apparent that while biblical laments appeal to God for help, they also serve to let the community—and by their preservation for posterity, the world—know of injustices. The plea, therefore, is not just to God; it is to fellow human beings, who upon learning of the injustice, are asked to respond with compassionate justice.

Job's Long-Suffering, and Impatient, Lament

> I will give free utterance to my complaint; I will speak in
> the bitterness of my soul. (Job 10:1)[7]

The biblical book of Job is enormously long. Here, we can only introduce the ways in which it participates in the lament tradition, contributes to it, and also innovates it, as well as some subsequent influences it has had on more contemporary theological grapplings with disaster and severe suffering.[8]

The story of Job in the Bible is well-known.[9] It is the story of a man who suffers grave losses in a series of terrible ordeals: marauding enemies capture his livestock, his servants and all ten of his children die from a natural storm disaster, and Job himself is stricken with a disease. Job is not aware of the heavenly council where God actually prompted the "satan" (meaning "accuser" or "tester" in Hebrew) to consider Job's faithfulness and goodness. The satan responded with a challenge to God—that Job is only faithful to God because everything has always gone his way; nothing bad has ever happened to him. The satan claims it has been easy for Job to believe in God, but his faith is only skin-deep, so to speak. So God allows the satan to test Job with these trials, confident that Job will not lose his faith when he suffers, and that Job will remain loyal to God.[10] The reader is privy to all this and will watch how Job responds.[11]

When the satan has completed the devastating hardships against Job, Job sits in shock and mourning from all his losses. His friends come to be with him, but follow a customary time of silence, refraining from speaking to him. Soon enough they will begin their talk, but it will be the wrong kinds of words, and overreaching explanations, to offer to one so stricken with grief. Essentially, the three "friends" all believe in an idea (a theology or ideology) found in parts of the Hebrew Bible (some psalms and proverbs, and some prophetic texts): that if a person or community experienced suffering, they must have done something wrong, or sinned; their state of hardship is a sign that they are being punished by God. This is a version of "retributive justice." Meanwhile, Job will go from minimal speech and self-expression at the outset, to an avalanche of words across several dozen chapters of the book.[12]

But Eliphaz first says to Job, after Job's extreme lament in which he wishes that he had never been born (Jeremiah had uttered a similar kind of lament; Jer 20:14-18):

> If one ventures a word with you, will you be offended?
> But who can keep from speaking?
> . . . Think now, who that was innocent ever perished?

Or where were the upright cut off?
As I have seen, those who plow iniquity
and sow trouble reap the same. . . . (Job 4:2, 7-8)

Initially, Job believes this traditional idea, that God is punishing him for some wrong, as indicated in his words below. Here Job asks that God would simply end his life and his suffering:

For the arrows of the Almighty are in me;
my spirit drinks their poison;
the terrors of God are arrayed against me. . . .
O that I might have my request,
and that God would grant my desire;
that it would please God to crush me,
that he would let loose his hand and cut me off! (Job 6:4, 8-9)

Job not only laments his own particular miseries. From his experience, he now extrapolates about all humanity; a once highly successful and privileged man, he begins to show an empathy with the lot and suffering of servants:

Do not human beings have a hard service on earth,
and are not their days like the days of a laborer?
Like a slave who longs for the shadow,
and like laborers who look for their wages,
so I am allotted months of emptiness,
and nights of misery are apportioned to me. . . .
Therefore, I will not restrain my mouth;
I will speak in the anguish of my spirit;
I will complain in the bitterness of my soul. (Job 7:1-3, 11)

As many commentators have noticed, Job soon takes the lyrics of a familiar psalm of praise that extols God's creation, and humankind's place of dominion in it (Ps 8:4: "What is man, that thou art mindful of him? and the son of man, that thou visitest him?"),[13] and parodies the psalm into a sarcastic lament to God:

What are human beings, that you make so much of them,
that you set your mind on them,

visit them very morning, test them every moment?
Will you not look away from me for a while?
leave me alone so I can swallow my spit?[14]
If I sin, what do I do to you,
you watcher of humanity?
Why have you made me your target?
Why have I become a burden to you?
Why do you not pardon my transgression . . . ? (Job 7:17-21)

Job raises the repeated questions we have seen previously in the lament prayer genre to a whole new level in his strident, honest complaint against God. Lament psalmists often appeal to God to "look!" and see their suffering. Job now ironically says he *does not want to be* the center of God's attention. We will see in the end, however, that God is not presented as having a problem with Job's words! God's long response to Job displaces him from the center of the created order. Moreover, in Job 42:7, God says to Job's friend, Eliphaz: "My wrath is kindled against you and against your two friends; for you have not spoken of me what is right, as my servant Job has." One can only surmise that God would rather have critical language aimed at God's own self, from a person who is in genuine relationship with him, than pseudo-pious language from the friends whose relationship with God is, in fact, superficial and simplistic. The friends' ideology vastly reduces God to a punisher of the bad and a rewarder of the good, and nothing more, while justifying themselves over against those who suffer. Job sees cracks in their theory, of course, that the evildoers are not always punished, and he laments: "Why do the wicked live on, reach old age, and grow mighty in power? . . . Their houses are safe from fear, and no rod of God is upon them . . . their children dance around" (Job 21:7, 9, 11b).

As the long, lyrical debate with his friends wears on, Job finds growing confidence in his belief that, while he is admittedly human and may have overlooked a failing of his own, he simply has not done anything wrong that deserves such punishment from God. In this evolution, we see the transformative power of lament in expressing one's self, the integrity of one's suffering, and an affirmation of personhood. In South Africa, laments in the book of Job are being used in pastoral care and group work with persons suffering from HIV/AIDS and the associated social stigma, to help process their suffering with compassion, in contrast to the traditional notion of a God who punishes with illness. The social-theological role of funerals is also recognized as extremely important in dealing with the HIV/AIDS crisis.[15]

Yet, Job still blames God for his hardships, as he is still in the grip of the traditional theology of divine cause for suffering. In chapter 16, Job gives a long list of all God's negative actions against him, reminiscent of the lamenters' complaint in the book of Lamentations that God treated them as though God were their enemy. Yet in the end, Job simply has no choice but to keep crying out to God, who is his only hope:

> My face is red with weeping,
> and deep darkness is on my eyelids,
> though there is no violence in my hands,
> and my prayer is pure.
> O earth, do not cover my blood;
> let my outcry find no resting place.
> Even now, in fact, my witness is in heaven,
> and he that vouches for me is on high. (Job 16:16-19)

Job despairs, but does not give up. He appeals to Earth, as an ally, not to conceal his blood, but to let his cry rise, so seeking empathy, just as innocent Abel and the Hebrew children in Egypt did, who received a compassionate hearing from God and then divine intervention. Job has nothing left but to believe in the God who freely acted in history and tradition.

Job wants a "hearing" with God, a conversation, so that God can fill him in on what he has done wrong to deserve such hardship. Just as God had the prophets bring a legal case in their rhetoric against the people of Israel, now Job ironically asks for the same, calling for God to make it known to him what his guilt is (Job 31:35). Moreover, Job at times sounds as though he would like to turn the tables on God, the judge, and bring God to trial to defend what the deity is doing. Such an extraordinary reversal is at play in the recent dramatization in film of prisoners in Auschwitz, who bring God to trial for his failures.[16]

After many long speeches by Job and the friends, God finally "answers" Job out of the whirlwind. However, God does not really answer Job's questions or concerns as to why he is suffering. God embarks on long, intimidating, overwhelming speeches about God's work as the great Creator, and all that God has created. God seems to ignore Job's challenge and argument, and chooses not to engage its content at all, while at the same time speaking to Job. To make matters worse, God keeps repeating to Job, "Where were you when I created all these things? If you know so much. . . ." God speaks of creating everything under the sun, including the animals, and finally only toward the end of the speech mentions human beings, as though they are not so important.

What are we to make of this book's engagement with the lament tradition? Clearly Job laments, long and hard, yet as was just mentioned, God does not directly answer his concerns. God chooses not to engage the line of reasoning, perhaps regarding it as not worth the time of day. Job has used the complaint element of the lament against God, who is treating him badly, he believes, for no reason. Job does get a "hearing" from God; God does respond to him, acknowledges him. God just doesn't give him the answer he demands, and instead seems to have a need to defend himself—God, that is. Neither does God deny that Job suffers, nor does God deny there are forces on the earth and in human existence that cause suffering. Perhaps Job's simply receiving a response in itself is enough. Those who experience the severest suffering or persecution often feel alone or abandoned, yet long to be heard and recognized. Getting a hearing from another human being can be transformative and empowering—and much more so if it is from God. God recognizes Job's voice and presence, and certainly changes, reorients, and enlarges Job's perspective. In effect, the cosmic perspective lifts Job out of his despair and preoccupation with (the traditional, insufficient explanation of) his suffering. Job is repositioned and restored in God's expansive world that has divine purpose and is good, the order of which is trustworthy and a subject of wonder. God takes Job along on a rhetorical sweep of God's grand vista and perspective and begins to transform Job's lament into wonder and praise. Not only this, but by giving Job more children at the story's end, without diminishing the real grief of loss, God restores to him personally a meaningful present and future—a tangible hope: he can live again.

If the book of Job, especially its long middle section, were refashioned for a postexilic context, we can see how the questions Job raises are, indirectly, the questions with which the exilic community struggled. The questions of why the innocent suffer, and why God causes or allows this—these were already foreshadowed in the book of Lamentations, but are picked up again in Job and taken a long way further. In sum, we can say that the book of Job shows that lament is not simply about asking for, and receiving, a demanded answer or simple explanation. Lament is about being acknowledged by God, and affirmed—along broader lines, about God seeing the unjust perpetrators. And yet lament in Job is also about how a lamenter may eventually need to be redirected away from what sorely preoccupies him or her, so as to transform, empower, and resume one's fuller humanity—to complete, or at least find resolution with, the grieving process, get past the embitterment, and get on with living.

Historic and Contemporary Laments of the People

Let us now consider some examples of historic and contemporary lament prayers, poems, and songs from Jewish-related tradition that exhibit some of the features discussed above—a description of distress, a human appeal for help, and a longing for answers and intervention. The horrors of genocide can lead survivors to a dark abyss where faith and hope grow dim, as this lament poem from the Holocaust suggests:

God of Mercy
Kadya Molodovsky

O God of Mercy
For the time being
Choose another people.
We are tired of death, tired of corpses,

We have no more prayers.
For the time being
Choose another people.
We have run out of blood
For victims,
Our houses have been turned into desert,
The earth lacks space for tombstones,
There are no more lamentations
Nor songs of woe
In the ancient texts. . . .[17]

While some persons of faith may find such stridency of complaint against God in lament prayers to be bordering on sacrilege or
blasphemy, the traditions of faith, poetry, and song across cultures
suggest instead that such extremes of appeal to God are indeed
expressions of the profoundest faith. These are individuals pushed
to the edge, and beyond, of disaster and unjust oppression, who can
be utterly honest with their God in a mature relationship without
fear or care of consequence.

At the same time, others in the context of the Holocaust, while
also expressing anger or near hopeless despair, have been able still to
raise timeworn, audacious lament prayer to God, as in this excerpt
from the conclusion of A. M. Klein's "Elegy":

. . .
Look down, O Lord, from thy abstracted throne!
Look down! Find out this Sodom to the sky
Rearing and solid on a world atilt
The architecture by its pillars known . . .
See where the pyramids
Preserve our ache between their angled tons:
Pass over, they have been excelled . . .
But do not overlook, oh pass not over
The hollow monoliths. The vengeful eye
Fix on these pylons of the sinister sigh,
The well-kept chimneys daring towards the sky!
From them, now innocent, no fumes do rise . . .
As Thou didst do to Sodom, do to them!

. . . Vengeance is thine, O Lord, and unto us
In a world wandering, amidst raised spears
Between wild waters, and against barred doors,
There are no weapons left. Where now but force
prevails, and over the once blest lagoons
Mushroom new Sinais, sole defensive is
The face turned east, and the uncompassed prayer.
Not prayer for the murdered myriads who
Themselves white liturgy before Thy throne
Are of my prayer; but for the scattered bone
Stirring in Europe's camps, next kin of death,
My supplication climbs the carboniferous air.
Grant them Ezekiel's prophesying breath!
Isaiah's cry of solacing allow!
. . . Oh, for Thy promise and Thy pity, now
At last, this people to its lowest brought
Preserve! Only in Thee our faith . . .
Thou only art responseful.

Hear me, who stand
Circled and winged in vortex of my kin:
Forgo the complete doom! The winnowed, spare!
Annul the scattering, and end!
. . . Towered Jerusalem and Jacob's tent
Set up again; again renew our days
As when near Carmel's mount we harbored ships,
And went and came, and knew our home; and song
From all the vineyards raised its sweet degrees,
And Thou didst visit us, didst shield from wrong,
And all our sorrows salve with prophecies;
Again renew them as they were of old,
And for all time cancel that ashen orbit
In which our days, and hopes, and kin, are rolled.[18]

In the 1960s in the United States, the music of Bob Dylan was noted for its prophetic lament for social injustice. Two examples will have to suffice. Bob Dylan wrote a song, "The Death of Emmett Till," to draw national attention to the grave injustice of the lynching of a boy from Chicago.[19] The second was a famous anti-war song about U.S. involvement in Vietnam, which, like the biblical lament psalms, raised many questions that remain unanswered.

Blowin' in the Wind

Bob Dylan

> . . . Yes, 'n' how many seas must a white dove sail
> Before she sleeps in the sand?

> . . . Yes, 'n' how many ears must one man have
> Before he can hear people cry?[20]

New Testament Lament as Prayerful Plea

> My God, My God, why have you forsaken me?
> (Matt 27:46b)

While it may appear initially that the lament form is absent or diminished in the New Testament,[21] it is important to remember that the earliest Christians, who were Jewish, revered the Torah, Prophets, and Psalms, just as the gentiles who later joined the movement also adopted the scriptures of the community. There is no collection of psalms (and laments) "in" the New Testament, because they would have utilized the psalms collection(s). When we turn to consider lament prayer genres reflected in the New Testament, particularly in the life and death of Jesus portrayed through the gospels, a number of elements emerge.

In Jesus' birth story, as rendered in Matthew, the gospel writer suggests that the current political leader, a paranoid Herod the Great, would seek to kill the infant (Matt 2:13-23), a parallel to the way in which Moses' life was threatened by Pharaoh. Thus, from his birth, Jesus also embodies lament; he is caught up in the fray of human suffering, as Moses was. When his plan is foiled, Herod responds by ordering the killing of babies in Bethlehem. The author of Matthew then refers to another lament tradition—the voice of Rachel, in response to Herod's killing, weeping anew for her children (a quote from Jer 31:15). The intentional connection of Jesus with the figure of Moses is not only a link with the model prophet, suggesting that Jesus stood in the prophetic tradition, but it is a link with the outcry of the slaves' lament in Exodus. The lament of Rachel was previously connected to those who went into Babylonian exile, yet who would be saved by God again. Thus God's chosen servant, Jesus (regarded as God's unique son by Christians), would also bring liberation and comfort for those languishing in the first century C.E.

In the birth narrative of the Gospel of Luke, the lament prayers of both Elizabeth and Zechariah, and of Jesus' mother, Mary, are answered by God. In a very common biblical theme, Elizabeth and Zechariah had not been able to have children. An angel appears to Zechariah and says, "Do not be afraid, Zechariah, for your prayer has been heard. Your wife Elizabeth will bear you a son, and you will name him John. You will have joy and gladness, and many will rejoice at this birth. . . ." (Luke 1:13-14). Here is a clear movement from lament to praise. Elizabeth responds: "This is what the Lord has done for me when he looked favorably on me and took away the disgrace I have endured among my people" (Luke 1:25). As noted above, often in the lament psalms, the lamenter beseeches God to "show favor" (Hebrew: *khanan*) or mercy; this same concept appears in Elizabeth's words. It appears again in Mary's long song of praise (or Magnificat) that she offers in response to God's answering of her lament prayer. It is the longest speech by a female figure in Luke and Acts,[22] the gospel and its sequel, both by the same author, who was noted for highlighting a positive regard for women. Mary's lyrics are clearly in the tradition of Miriam and Hannah's lyrics (1 Sam 2:1-10) in the Hebrew Bible, who sang to God in thanks and praise for God's deliverance of the weak, poor, and oppressed (Jewish tradition also includes Hannah as one of seven women prophets in the Bible—including Miriam, Mary's namesake). Commentator Mary Foskett suggests that Mary is cast as a prophet in this text in Luke.[23] Traditional commentators have often suggested that these lyrics were not Mary's composed song, but that the words were put in her mouth from elsewhere. We have seen, however, the close connection between prophets and lament (in Moses, Miriam, Jeremiah, Second Isaiah, and elsewhere).

My soul magnifies the Lord,
and my spirit rejoices in God my Savior,
for he has looked with favor on the lowliness of his servant.
Surely, from now on all generations will call me blessed;
for the Mighty One has done great things for me,
and holy is his name.
His mercy is for those who fear him
from generation to generation.
He has shown strength with his arm;
he has scattered the proud in the thoughts of their hearts.
He has brought down the powerful from their thrones,
and lifted up the lowly;
he has filled the hungry with good things,
and sent the rich away empty.
He has helped his servant Israel,
in remembrance of his mercy,
according to the promise he made to our ancestors,
to Abraham and to his descendants forever. (Luke 1:46-55)

In the gospels, Jesus reaches out to the marginalized and to those persecuted who lamented, to give them comfort, liberation, and hope—including women,[24] Samaritans, gentiles, the sick, sinners, the poor, and the dead. Jesus resurrected at least two persons, the New Testament suggests, just as the prophet Elijah initiated resurrections centuries earlier. Jesus wept over the death of Lazarus before restoring him. He freed or healed those held captive by the ideology of retributive justice (like Job) that was still holding sway, which gave individuals no hope for a different future. The man born blind (John 9:1-41), who laments to Jesus for healing, is an example. At the beginning of his ministry, so the writer of Luke suggests, Jesus read in the synagogue from the scroll of Isaiah 42. Just as Second Isaiah portrayed a prophetic comforter who offered God's acceptance and a future to the people who were lamenting in exile, so the gospel writer suggests that Jesus fulfilled this role in his day for those languishing hopelessly.

The "Lord's Prayer" (Matt 6:9-13) that Jesus taught his disciples includes, in essence, the usual lament prayer elements. It does not elaborate on God's past saving actions or move to praise. Was it intended to be a static, unchanging prayer, or one that serves as a guide for improvisation, depending on one's circumstances?

> Our Father in heaven, [address]
> hallowed be your name. [divine attribute]
> Your kingdom come. [plea]
> Your will be done, [plea]
> on earth as it is in heaven.
> Give us this day our daily bread. [plea]
> And forgive us our debts, [confession]
> as we also have forgiven our debtors.
> And do not bring us to the time of trial, [plea]
> but rescue us from the evil one. [plea][25]

Jesus provided comfort to his disciples at the Last Supper, those whose lament of anticipated grief at losing him would have been profound beyond measure.

> Very truly, I tell you, you will weep and mourn, but the world will rejoice; you will have pain, but your pain will turn into joy. When a woman is in labor, she has pain, because her hour has come. But when her child is born, she no longer remembers the anguish because of the joy of having brought a human being into the world. So you have pain now; but I will see you again, and your hearts will rejoice, and no one will take your joy from you. (John 16:20-22)

The above is reminiscent of numerous texts in the Hebrew Bible that speak of the shift from sadness to joy, such as in Psalm 30:5b, 11, where a lamenter gives thanks for God's transformation of his or her illness: "Weeping may linger for the night, but joy comes with the morning. . . . You [God] have turned my mourning into dancing; you have taken off my sackcloth and clothed me with joy." This phraseology is common within the comfort speeches of Second Isaiah.

On the other hand, what is sometimes called Jesus' "Lament over Jerusalem"—a brief text in Matt 23:37—is really Jesus' critique of the city of Jerusalem in the manner of the prophets who cried "woe" against it with a communal dirge as warning; in other words, his lament is because the leaders and people are refusing to change their ways in order to avoid disaster.

More significantly, according to William Holladay's analysis, psalms are quoted some 196 times in the New Testament.[26] These come from thirty-five psalms, and of these, nineteen are laments. Not only are the psalms' influence on the New Testament pervasive, the lament psalms are woven into the fabric of the texts with allusions (some less noticeable) and outright quotations. Thirteen of the nineteen laments include reference to the enemies' persecution, in line with the emphasis in the Hebrew Bible.

Significantly, when Peter sought to use violence and to exact retribution for a soldier's action against Jesus in Gethsemane, Jesus stopped him, in effect refusing to pursue vengeance for wrong against himself. Jesus recognized wrongs and injustices, and he aimed to free persons from persecution, but he replaced retribution with forgiveness. This marks a liberation from cycles of punishment and violence, a pattern still at work in the Exodus liberation story, yet a liberation already begun in the garden of Eden, when God did not execute Adam and Eve for disobedience, and spared Cain's life though he had taken Abel's. With Jesus, a willing sacrifice of death, instead, became redemptive. With his embodied lament, he *innovates* the crucial lament element that normally calls for vengeance/revenge against one's enemy by breaking the pattern and relinquishing revenge. This element of lament, then, is being transformed through the New Testament's use of the genre here, but this transformation was already well underway in earlier Hebrew scripture. Jesus simply carried forward his Jewish heritage in faithfulness to God's difficult call.

The most notable reuse of the laments in the New Testament is in the narratives of Jesus' suffering. This happened at the time of the Jewish Passover, with its emphasis on exodus suffering, the Haggadah's "Song of Moses" (Exod 15), the *hallel* (Pss 113–118), and Psalm 136. William Holladay notes the following lament psalms woven into the passion narrative: Psalm 31 ("into your hands I commit my spirit"), Psalm 35 ("they hated me without a cause"), Psalm 41 (reference to a friend who betrays), and Psalm 69 ("those who hate me without cause," as well as "zeal for your house" in reference to money-changers in the temple).[27] Jesus' outcry from the cross while he was being crucified was rendered in Matthew 27:46—"My God, my God, why have you forsaken me?" (alluding to a version of lament Psalm 22). His cry was not answered in the way that any individual would plead for: an avoidance or release from suffering. But Psalm 22 is one of the lament psalms, as passed down in the Psalter, for which the lamenter did receive God's saving intervention and rescue, as indicated by the verb shift in the very middle of 22:21: ". . . *save me* from the mouth of the lion! From the horns of the wild oxen *you have rescued me. . . .*"[28] The shift from lament to praise is suggestive for this tragedy. One can only surmise that though the gospel writer quoted just the first line of the psalm, a full version of it was in Jesus' consciousness. With the gospel writer, it would be inappropriate to fabricate speech from Jesus at such an auspicious, critical moment; it is more likely that the memory of his words that had been passed down was included in the retelling of the passion. But did Jesus know the outcome of his unfolding ordeal? With oral tradition, any psalm can be modified to suit new circumstances, as we have seen. The gospel also records that Jesus prayed a lament (three times) in the garden of Gethsemane, "not my will, but thine, O Lord" (Matt 26:39).[29] At what point did Jesus expect a transformation of his embodied lament by a rescue *from* God, or a restoration *to* God?

Not only are humans shown to participate in lament and longing for rescue and transformation, but so is the whole creation. At the crucifixion, the Gospel of Matthew notes "from noon on, darkness came over the whole land" just prior to Jesus' lament, and "the earth shook, and the rocks were split" (27:51); Luke adds "the sun's light failed" (23:45). In the period after Jesus' death, the apostle Paul suggested, "For the creation waits with eager longing for the revealing of the children of God . . . the creation itself will be set free from its bondage to decay and will obtain the freedom of the glory of the children of God" (Rom 8:19, 21).

Jesus' death, interpreted so monumentally and uniquely by Christian theology, might leave the reader wondering how we can relate. A more contemporary example, from 1838, might be seen in the Cherokee leader Tsali, an old man whose family, along with many others, was to be forcibly removed by the U.S. army from their homeland in the unfolding "Trail of Tears" episode. Thousands of Cherokee had already been sent west; about five thousand persons died en route (for thousands of years they had occupied forty thousand square miles over portions of what came to be eight Southern states). Tsali was wrongly accused by the army authorities of aiming to kill two of the soldiers while his family was trying to escape deeper into the southern Appalachian mountains. He was offered a deal. If he and his older sons turned themselves in to the authorities, without the opportunity for a trial, in order to face certain execution as retribution for the soldiers' deaths, the remaining families of his people not yet forcibly removed would be treated well and allowed to stay in their homeland. With no certainty that he could trust the promise, he agonizingly agreed. His sons were executed, and so was Tsali. His sacrificial death helped ensure a future for some of the "eastern band" of the Cherokee in North Carolina. He could have chosen to fight an endless cycle of a losing battle, albeit in righteous self-defense, having been treated unjustly. He chose the high ground, to the shame of the U.S. authorities to this day. His life and death are remembered, not as a warrior, but because he gave his life and died nobly for the good of his people.[30] While there are a number of renditions of a traditional Cherokee song, "On the trail where they cried,"[31] here is a Cherokee lament:

Children on the Trail

Issac Welch Jr.

Along the way are scattered the bones and dust
of thousands of people who lived in the way of the Earth.
Humble but proud. Like winds of the mountains,
the souls and spirits of generations were irrevocably
uprooted to be removed from the soils of their ancestors.

Following the stream of humanity out of the foggy mists of
the blue and on to the open and rolling valleys sweltering with
    heat.
Some children played and some cried.

Darkness found them exhausted and fitful in weary slumber
as the aches and pains of their young legs eased.
Gradually the fun ceased and was replaced by numbing misery.
The young aged and followed as the calf follows the cow.
Eventually some of them fell and were left to perish.

Listen . . . to the whispers of the willows.
You can hear the happy chatter of the children.
Listen . . . to the oaks and you can hear the sniffles
and silent whimpers of the weary children.
Reach . . . toward the horizons and you can feel
the pain and sorrow of the young.

The children, the children . . . the children. . . .[32]

Returning to the New Testament, one looks in vain at the description of Jesus' death to find a dirge sung—either there, or at the burial site. The writer of the Gospel of John, who tends to keep Jesus more aloof from the fray of his own suffering, renders him as walking the way of the cross and turning to the people mourning behind him, to "women who were beating their breasts and wailing for him." He says to them, "Daughters of Jerusalem, do not weep for me, but weep for yourselves and for your children . . . . ," perhaps suggestive of the devastations to come forty years later in the Roman destruction of the temple and the resulting Jewish diaspora. Apart from this, in the first century, there was a belief there would be a "general resurrection" at the end of time (cf. the comment of Martha to Jesus in John 11:24). Jesus' resurrection may have answered a human need for hope and promise of each individual's resurrection upon death. Perhaps his followers' belief in and experience of this resurrection—regarded not as a defeat, but a great victory over death—caused their shift in focus away from lament and the grief of his death. However, this absence of human lament for Jesus' death across the gospels is unfortunate, perhaps, as it seems to suggest a glossing over of the full suffering and transformation that he and his followers experienced. On the other hand, what of God's silence throughout Jesus' suffering and death? We have noted earlier that sometimes silence is the appropriate response in the face of immense suffering.

In looking further for lament in the Gospel accounts, Mary Magdalene's sorrow for Jesus would have been transformed directly by his encountering and addressing her at the garden tomb, and giving her a message of good news to share with the disciples, in place of the usual expected dirge song of his death that the women would have had to sing. On hearing the news, Jesus' mother, Mary, would have been transformed from heartbreaking grief for her son to the realization of his ongoing life. Indeed in this story, especially the experience of women—whom we have noted throughout history and across cultures have had to carry great burdens of lament—is transformed. Peter is relieved of the grief of having betrayed Jesus by the post-resurrection encounter in which Jesus asks him three times, "Do you love me?"

The most widely known post-biblical lament practice in the traditions of the early church developed around the commemoration of Jesus' passion (suffering) and death. The tenebrae service (c. fifth century), held over the three days of Holy Week before Easter, was marked by the extinguishing of lights and by narrative readings and a liturgy about Jesus' suffering. A widespread tradition of Mary's lament for Jesus (*planctus Mariae*) as the "Mother of Sorrow" also developed. In general, however, the church shifted the focus of the lament tradition, from the Hebrew Bible's priority on injustice and innocent suffering, to penitential laments emphasizing Jesus' redemptive suffering for sinners.

However, the old lament tradition was retained in the "spirituals" of slaves in America and the blues and subsequent "gospel" music of black churches. The spirituals were shaped not just by the exodus story but by other biblical rescue stories, by the lament psalms, by faith in Jesus as savior, and by African call-and-response patterns and rhythms that allow freedom of improvisation.[33] Perhaps the embodiment of this passionate and meaningful tradition is congruent with a similar vibrancy that must have existed in ancient Israel, as it produced a continuing, influential, living legacy, down through the millennia, of an array of liturgical and musical branches across cultures. But "the blues" were uniquely American, more secular, yet they complement the earlier sacred spirituals from which they grew. James Cone suggests both forms shared in the sacred; he called the blues "secular spirituals."[34]

The singer and actor Paul Robeson said,

> The power of spirit that our people have is intangible, but it is a great force that must be unleashed in the struggles of today. A spirit of steadfast determination, exaltation in the face of trials—it is the very soul of our people that has been formed through the long and weary years of our march toward freedom . . . That spirit lives in our people's songs—in the sublime grandeur of "Deep River," in the driving force of "Jacob's Ladder," in the militancy of "Joshua Fit the Battle of Jericho," and in the poignant beauty of all of our spirituals.[35]

This exaltation and praise described within the spirituals and blues, in the midst of the severest hardship, is like the feature observed in the psalms, of praise music offered in anticipation of help or in hopeful anticipation of something better.[36] Writer Albert Murray says, "There was a big difference between having the blues and playing the blues. Playing the blues was a matter of getting rid of the blues. The lyrics may have been tragic in their orientation, but the music was about having a good time. So the music was really a matter of stomping the blues away."[37] This is why saxophonist Branford Marsalis can say,

> The blues are about freedom, you know. There's liberation in reality. When they talk about these songs, when they talk about being sad, the fact that you recognize, the fact that you recognize that which pains you is a very freeing and liberating experience . . . It must be strange for other cultures where you spend most of your time trying to pretend like you don't have any of these problems . . . When I hear the blues, the blues makes me smile.[38]

As the PBS series notes, "Over the next century, the blues would become the underground aquifer that would feed all the streams of American music, including jazz," and would influence music around the world.[39]

The importance of spirituals being sung in community is indicated by the words of the traditional spiritual "Couldn't Hear Nobody Pray," implying a solitary escape to freedom.

Couldn't Hear Nobody Pray

An' I couldn't hear nobody pray.
O Lord!
Couldn't hear nobody pray,
O way down yonder
By myself,
I couldn't hear nobody pray,

In the valley,
Couldn't hear nobody pray,
On my knees,
Couldn't hear nobody pray,
With my burden,
Couldn't hear nobody pray,
An' my Savior,
Couldn't hear nobody pray.

O Lord!

I couldn't hear nobody pray,
O Lord!
Couldn't hear nobody pray.
O way down yonder
By myself,
I couldn't hear nobody pray.

Chilly waters,
Couldn't hear nobody pray,
In the Jordan,
Couldn't hear nobody pray,
Crossing over,
Couldn't hear nobody pray.
Into Canaan,
Couldn't hear nobody pray.

O Lord!

I couldn't hear nobody pray,
O Lord!
Couldn't hear nobody pray.
O way down yonder
By myself,
I couldn't hear nobody pray.

Hallejuh!
Couldn't hear nobody pray,
Troubles over,
Couldn't hear nobody pray,
In the Kingdom,
Couldn't hear nobody pray,
With my Jesus,
Couldn't hear nobody pray.

O Lord!

I couldn't hear nobody pray,
O Lord!
Couldn't hear nobody pray.
O way down yonder
By myself,
I couldn't hear nobody pray.[40]

Bernice Johnson Reagon, civil rights singer, founder of the group Sweet Honey in the Rock, and musicologist, spent her career leading workshops to keep the spirituals and songs of the civil rights movement alive for black congregations and a new generation. She has said of her approach to music:

I'm basically a 19th century singer, which means that I'm not a soloist. . . . Singing does not make sense to me without the congregation. The singing exists to form the community. In Western formal choral tradition, there's an aim for a blend so you cannot distinguish where the parts are coming from. With congregational singing, I could drive up to the church and they could be singing and I could tell you who was there, because the individual timbres of a voice never disappear.[41]

Excerpts of Reagon's teaching and singing of spirituals, along with Bill Moyers's interview of her, can be found on the PBS website from "The Songs are Free" program.[42]

Thomas A. Dorsey, considered the "father of gospel," in the words of Melva W. Costen "was a pioneer in fusing instrumental accompaniments clearly associated with forms created outside the church . . . quite rhythmic, 'bluesy,' highly syncopated. . . ."[43] In 1932 Dorsey wrote the words to "Precious Lord, Take My Hand," a lament prayer in the genre of the psalms. He wrote it in Chicago after the traumatic experience of his wife's death and a tragic stillbirth. Leaving a revival church service in St. Louis, he said, "People were happily singing and clapping around me, but I could hardly keep from crying out." He went home, made it through the funerals, but then withdrew from family, friends, and music. "I felt that God had done me an injustice. I didn't want to serve him anymore or write gospel songs. I just wanted to go back to that jazz world I once knew so well," he said. A friend encouraged him to go in a room with a piano. There he felt God's comforting presence and received inspiration for the words and music of "Precious Lord, Take my Hand."[44] Many years later, Mahalia Jackson offered a profound performance of the song at the funeral of Martin Luther King Jr. in 1968.[45]

Precious Lord, Take My Hand

Thomas A. Dorsey

Precious Lord, take my hand,
Lead me on, let me stand,
I am tired, I am weak, I am worn;
Through the storm, through the night,
Lead me on to the light:

Refrain:
Take my hand, precious Lord,
Lead me home.

When my way grows drear,
Precious Lord, linger near,

When my life is almost gone,
Hear my cry, hear my call,
Hold my hand lest I fall:

Refrain

When the darkness appears
And the night draws near,
And the day is past and gone,
At the river I stand,
Guide my feet, hold my hand:
Refrain [46]

Contemporary American popular music that has some linkage to the stream of spirituals, blues, and jazz in their oral improvisational element includes rap and hip-hop. Many hip-hop performers, however, glorify some of the negative and destructive features of urban life and do not carry the legacy forward. Yet there are other performers whose work can be regarded as striving to retrieve the social concern and justice element of the ancient lament and prophetic traditions and of the spirituals and blues. This alternative hip-hop cries out as a social critique, a description of distress like the lament psalms, an ethical and spiritual message. Some of the work of the artists—Mos Def, Talib Kweli, Common, Lupe Fiasco, Lauryn Hill—fits this bill. [47] Common's song "I Have a Dream" is a tribute to Martin Luther King Jr., seeking inspiration and guidance for today's urban needs. [48] Lauryn Hill's performance, with Ziggy Marley, of "Redemption Song" is a tribute to Jamaican Bob Marley's monumental musical influence; it speaks directly to the role of freedom songs to convey positive values of love and peace in liberation movements. [49]

The Beatles' 1970 song "Let It Be" is about answered lament. Mary, mother of Jesus, offers consoling comfort to the singer. This is not uncommon, of course, within the Roman Catholic tradition where, especially among the laity, persons appeal to Mary as an intercessor on their behalf when they suffer.

Let It Be

The Beatles

When I find myself in times of trouble
Mother Mary comes to me
Speaking words of wisdom, let it be . . .[50]

More recently, blues performer Eric Clapton and the late opera singer Luciano Pavarotti combined to perform the song "Holy Mother" with a gospel choir. The song is also a lament prayer; apart from the lyrics of suffering, as in the blues and gospel traditions, the music moves from lament to praise as the arrangement unfolds. Pavarotti organized and performed in humanitarian concerts with many others over the years to draw attention to the needs of people suffering in war.

Holy Mother

Eric Clapton and Stephen Bishop

Holy mother, hear my prayer,
Somehow I know you're still there. . . .[51]

Not every lament claims a religious heritage or background, and a lament may critique the religious who are oblivious to suffering. Mazisi Kunene, Poet Laureate of South Africa, wrote of those who go along not hearing the people's cry.

They Also Are Children of the Earth

Mazisi Kunene

Cursed shall be the one whose passage in this world
Evades humaneness, engenders greed and hoarding
Cursed is he wallowing alone in caskets of wealth and
Counting rosary beads of accumulated cars
To be human is to humbly cherish the sweat of your toil
In measured style of decency and appreciation
To be human is to consider the plight of the needy

As they also are children of the earth
Yes, men and women of this blessed land.[52]

In South Africa, the terrible ordeal and abuses of the white apartheid regime against blacks, and its final dismantling, unfolded before the world's eyes. South African poet Mzi Mahola lamented the awful treatment of blacks by the authorities, describing a scene that was carried out countless times throughout the country before change came:

What Will They Eat?

Mzi Mahola

There was stormy panic
When the police came
To round up polltax defaulters.
Once more the knowing forest
Hurriedly beckoned
To hide in its bosom
Men of the village.
But uncle was again betrayed
By his arthritic limbs.
Women wailed
Hearts seized by apprehension
And cousin cried
Fear in his little heart.
We had never seen a handcuffed person.

The police returned one day
And we craned our necks for uncle.
But he was not there.
For a long time,
Lasting almost the day,
Grandpa and grandma
Argued with the white policemen.
There was a black one
Well known for torturing

Standing away near the kraal
Like a skullpanda.

For the first time I saw tears
In granny's dark face,
Grandpa so furious
It was coming through his nose.
That day no tea,
Cookies or sour milk were served.
In the afternoon the guests left.
Granny was in grief
Parroting a recital,
"What will they eat?
What will my children eat?"

In the evening a man came
To herd all three suckling cattle,
Their calves and a pregnant cow.
He drove them away.
He herded away our wealth,
Our source of nutrition,
Grandfather's status and pride.
Their value would pay for his son's freedom.
A complete invalid.

Grief was choking my throat.
Would they know their special names?
Would they graze them in lucerne?
Give them chaff and salt?
What of the green acres at home?
The calabashes,
Would they now be turned upside down?
What would we milk, feed the dogs on?
We would never again
Watch them grazing in the field.

For many seasons
Our home lay

Under the roof of sorrow.
Now I know
That from a dog's withered back
You can tell that
There's hunger in a home.[53]

In 1990, Desmond Tutu was interviewed following the release of Nelson Mandela after twenty-seven years in prison. He was asked, "What does this release mean for the black South African community and South Africa in general?" He responded, "It is saying to us, God hears . . . God acts, God is really involved. We've been praying so long and it seemed like our prayers were just going into a void. Now [what we prayed for] is happening and we are getting hope that we are going to be free, all the people in this land, not just black people, the white people are not free either. . . ."[54] Addressing a crowd gathered at St. George's Cathedral after Mandela's address to the public, Archbishop Tutu said,

> Sometimes, after all that has happened in our country, we might have been forgiven for wondering whether God was around, whether God saw, whether God heard, whether God was aware of the suffering, the injustice, the oppression. People detained, jailed, tortured. People exiled, people killed. All of this, it seemed, did not touch God. God seemed indifferent or God was weak. . . . These words, which we sometimes quoted, of the Lord saying to his people, "I have witnessed the misery of my people in Egypt, and have heard them crying out because of their oppressors. I know what they are suffering and have come down to rescue them"— those words seemed such a mockery. . . . Do you remember the funerals that we have had? . . . God is in charge, we said. Maybe sometimes it was like whistling in the dark to keep up our courage. Then . . . you remember how I used to say [unjust rulers] will bite the dust? . . . We have seen some extraordinary things, haven't we? . . . So we have come here to say thank you, God, that you are in fact a God who . . . comes down to deliver your people. We thank you, God, that you have been on the side of those who have been oppressed. We thank God, too, for our overseas partners and friends who have supported and continue to support our struggle

with their prayers, with their pressure, with their sanctions. . . .
And so, friends, we have come to give thanks [for] the beginning
of the end of apartheid, the dawn of a new South Africa. We come
to give thanks to God for the possibilities about which we have
been dreaming that we seem to be realizing. God bless you and
God protect you.[55]

Since 1994, millions of South Africans continue to wait for
the alleviation of vast poverty. The following excerpt of a poem by
Vonani Bila shows and quietly laments the kind of poverty in which
many people live who have yet to benefit materially from the new
South Africa.

A Visit to Oom Brown

Vonani Bila

a visit to the squatter camp
takes months of preparation.
gathering of coins, courage and small heartily big gifts.

oom brown lives in cold broken-down hammanskraal
i climb and change old kombis[56] from elim,
makhado, polokwane, mokopane, modimolle
squashed
to meet oom brown
before he kicks the bucket.

he lives in a corrugated iron house
with one cat that chases rats, two unfed dogs and three goats
he warms his feet and hands around the brazier
he and his old wife talk about life's empty harvest.

we eat fried peanuts
fired in a small old three-legged pot
in a grass-thatched hut.
gogo tsatsawani brings a plate of pap and masonja,
i wash my hands in a bowl of warm water,
eat dinner with pleasure.

around the fire
oom brown tells tales of dispossession,
"i fought during the second world war
while the boers received tracts of fertile land
they gave me an old bicycle."
he tells tales as he finishes a plastic carton of beer.
he advises me how to live life . . .

he says i must chew muti to be a lion:
. . . muti for dignity when i talk to authority
muti to live beyond eighty years
muti every time i wake up, walk in the day, and when i sleep.

oom brown's wife's eyes close slowly.
she wraps herself in a rag,
whispers in my ears,
"oom brown is no good;
sometimes he transforms into a snake, lion, hyena.
the comrades cannot touch him."
oom brown coughs strenuously,
he quivers,
twists his lips,
talks in tongues like a miracle man.
surely something in the blood reminds him
of the zombified children, boys, girls, men and women,
who toil day and night in his tobacco fields.

gogo tsatsawani speaks out loud:
"we warm ourselves like this every night;
around the fire
we watch the stars until morning.
the shack is cold. . . ."[57]

Returning to America, we find the poetry of Ruth Faulkner Grubbs, who grew up in Whitley County, Kentucky. In two poems, she writes of the beauty of her people in Appalachia, and quietly laments the deprivations of poverty through many generations.

Black Oak (a place)

Ruth Faulkner Grubbs

She lived there, my mother's mother,
Mommie to me,
in a board and batten house
standing 100 years on the hill.
There we watched, past the holler,
into the pasture field where jerseys grazed
and left cow piles rich to feed the red soil
around tomatoes and corn
that grew down the steep bank to the well.

We watched into the field where dandelion greens
and crow's feet and mouse's ears and dock grew
to fill the black iron pots with salat to eat
with flat cakes of cornpone at supper time.

We watched past the field and the railroad
to Jellico, the Kentucky side,
hanging on a hill between Pine Mountain
and 25 W winding its way to Williamsburg.
Where shanties and the Texaco station soaked in
dust along side the calaboose holding prisoners
to go tomorrow to the country seat for hearing
their fate for moonshinin or breaking in
to steal a way of feedin their young-uns and gettin by.

Back across the bottom fields rich
with river dirt from the lazy creek that would rage
full grown and fast with heavy summer rains
we watched ponderous jaws of steel chew holes
and grab soil and the grass and grains of life
of new beginnings of all the seasons to come.
Strip minin, they called it, black gold.
To fire engines and stoves in factories
to build more things, they said, a different kind of beauty.

They left, and the holes filled with water
and lured young boys, some to swim
and some to drown.[58]

Mommie

Ruth Faulkner Grubbs

I see her now, the long front porch
ragged rails and raw plank flooring
walking stooped to the willow rocker.

She sits with her bible
preaching duty and sin to her grandchildren.

I see hands thin and wrinkled
that work like instruments of precision
small finger bent to neat hook
a gift from her ancestors
stringing and breaking beans
peeling potatoes, peeling apples
to dry in the hot summer sun.

Shift dress from four sacks
bun of hair held in place
a hairpin color of red-eye gravy.

My little Babe, she called me
maybe her favorite girl child
(she loved the boy more
the only one among girls)
and said, she'll be a nurse.
I didn't want it but it happened that way.[59]

The Qur'an and Lament in Prayer

Sura 14:39

Praise be to Allah,[60] Who hath granted unto me in old
age Isma'il and Isaac: for truly my Lord is He, the Hearer
of Prayer!

Some examples of lament poems, popular prayers, and songs have already been shared from Muslim cultures around the world. Most prayer in Islam falls into three types: the ritual obligatory prayer offered five times per day (*salāt*); the remembering/invoking/repetition of God's name and attributes (*dhikr*); and supplication (*du'ā'*), which is the basic lament prayer genre we have been discussing.[61]

When we turn to the Qur'an, which unites all Muslims in their faith, prayer is a central feature in the text, which also institutes obligatory prayer.[62] As the Qur'an is Allah's revelation to the holy prophet Muhammad,[63] it is essentially divine communication with him, so that prayer and meditation receive great importance. Prayer and action by Muslim believers after the model of Muhammad are centrally important in Islam.

The following quotations of suras (chapters) from a translation of the Qur'an include many of the passages that address prayer, and most of them concern the experience of calling to the deity for help as supplication. Muslims will be familiar with these suras, but the numerous excerpts are included here for others who are less familiar with the Qur'an. As will be seen, many references to texts and people found in the Bible appear in the Qur'an, such as Moses and Job, and a number of these references relate to lament prayer.[64] Every sura (of the total 114) begins with the line: "In the name of Allah, Most Gracious, Most Merciful."

The Opening (al-Fatiha) of the Qur'an below not only alludes to the core practice of prayer, including supplication to God for help ("Thine aid do we seek"), as suggested in *ayah* five (*ayah* = verse), but the very core of what we have called "lament prayer"—the plea—appears in verse six with the following specific appeal: "show us the straight way." Moreover, the Fatiha is recited seventeen times daily across the five obligatory prayers (*salāt*) by Muslims. Most translations give the end of verse five along the lines of "to You do we pray for help," or "ask/implore/beg/beseech for help," or, "seek aid." As Michael Sells has recently shown to a wider audience by way of his book *Approaching the Qur'an: The Early Revelations*, the matter of the virtuosity of reciters of the Qur'an and *salāt* in Muslim communities worldwide is evident by the many audio and video recordings one might listen to on CDs or the Internet today.[65] The following excerpts from Abdullah Yusuf Ali's translation of the Qur'an show the importance of prayer and its supplication or lament element.[66] The chapter (sura) names for each excerpt are given in English with transliterated Arabic. God often speaks not with "I" but with the subject pronoun "We," explained as "the plural of majesty."

Sura 1:5, Opening (al-Fatiha)

(1) In the name of Allah, Most Gracious, Most Merciful.

(2) Praise be to Allah, the Cherisher and Sustainer of the worlds;

(3) Most Gracious, Most Merciful;

(4) Master of the Day of Judgment.

(5) Thee do we worship, and Thine aid we seek.

(6) Show us the straight way,

(7) The way of those on whom Thou hast bestowed Thy Grace, those whose (portion) is not wrath, and who go not astray.

Sura 2:60, The Cow (al-Baqarah)

And remember Moses prayed for water for his people; We said: "Strike the rock with thy staff." Then gushed forth therefrom twelve springs. Each group knew its own place for water. So eat and drink of the sustenance provided by Allah, and do no evil nor mischief on the (face of the) earth.

The following excerpt shows the importance to the faithful of showing compassion for those who suffer, including the weak and marginal and oppressed ones, as also seen in the Hebrew Bible and New Testament. Prayer is closely linked with practicing charity.

Sura 2:177

It is not righteousness that ye turn your faces towards east or west; but it is righteousness to believe in Allah and the Last Day, and the Angels, and the Book, and the Messengers; to spend of your substance, out of love for Him, for your kin, for orphans, for the needy, for the wayfarer, for those who ask, and for the ransom of slaves; to be steadfast in prayer, and practice regular charity; to fulfil the contracts which ye have made; and to be firm and patient, in pain (or suffering) and adversity, and throughout all periods of panic. Such are the people of truth, the Allah-fearing.

Sura 2:186 (listen through the link on the companion website)

When My servants ask thee concerning Me, I am indeed close (to them): I listen to the prayer of every suppliant when he calleth on Me: Let them also, with a will, listen to My call, and believe in Me: That they may walk in the right way.

Sura 2:238-239

(238) Guard strictly your (habit of) prayers, especially the Middle Prayer; and stand before Allah in a devout (frame of mind).

(239) If ye fear (an enemy), pray on foot, or riding, (as may be most convenient), but when ye are in security, celebrate Allah's praises in the manner He has taught you, which ye knew not (before).

The following sura affirms that God delivers persons from danger, and it shows a practice similar to that seen in the other traditions, that once having been delivered, the person who prayed follows with gratitude and by fulfilling their "vow" of praise to God.

Sura 6:63-64, The Cattle (al-An'am)

(63) Say: "Who is it that delivereth you from the dark recesses of land and sea, when ye call upon Him in humility and silent terror: 'If He only delivers us from these (dangers), (we vow) we shall truly show our gratitude'?"

(64) Say "It is Allah that delivereth you from these and all (other) distresses: and yet ye worship false gods!"

In this next sura, Abraham is remembered as having compassionately lamented in prayer for a city, and an emphasis that is not seen in the Bible is added in the Qur'an, that Abraham is especially keen to have his offspring practice prayer, which he has known to be so important.

Sura 14:35-41, Abraham (Ibrahim)

(35) Remember Abraham said: "O my Lord! make this city one of peace and security: and preserve me and my sons from worshipping idols."

(36) "O my Lord! they have indeed led astray many among mankind; He then who follows my (ways) is of me, and he that disobeys me—but Thou art indeed Oft-forgiving, Most Merciful."

(37) "O our Lord! I have made some of my offspring to dwell in a valley without cultivation, by Thy Sacred House; in order, O our Lord, that they may establish regular Prayer: so fill the hearts of some among men with love towards them, and feed them with fruits: so that they may give thanks."

(38) "O our Lord! truly Thou dost know what we conceal and what we reveal: for nothing whatever is hidden from Allah, whether on earth or in heaven."

(39) "Praise be to Allah, Who hath granted unto me in old age Isma'il and Isaac: for truly my Lord is He, the Hearer of Prayer!"

(40) "O my Lord! make me one who establishes regular Prayer, and also (raise such) among my offspring O our Lord! and accept Thou my Prayer."

(41) "O our Lord! cover (us) with Thy Forgiveness—me, my parents, and (all) Believers, on the Day that the Reckoning will be established!"

The following sura includes a litany of persons of faith, under the heading "prophets," most of whom are also found in the Hebrew Bible and New Testament, who lamented to God and whose prayers were answered.

Sura 21:76, 83-91, The Prophets (al-Anbiya')

(76) (Remember) Noah, when he cried (to Us) aforetime: We listened to his (prayer) and delivered him and his family from great distress. . . .

(83) And (remember) Job, when He cried to his Lord, "Truly distress has seized me, but Thou art the Most Merciful of those that are merciful."

(84) So We listened to him: We removed the distress that was on him, and We restored his people to him, and doubled their number—as a Grace from Ourselves, and a thing for commemoration, for all who serve Us.

(85) And (remember) Isma'il, Idris, and Zul-kifl, all (men) of constancy and patience;

(86) We admitted them to Our mercy: for they were of the righteous ones.

(87) And remember Zun-nun [Jonah], when he departed in wrath: He imagined that We had no power over him! But he cried through the depths of darkness, "There is no god but thou: glory to thee: I was indeed wrong!"

(88) So We listened to him: and delivered him from distress: and thus do We deliver those who have faith.

(89) And (remember) Zakariya [Zechariah], when he cried to his Lord: "O my Lord! leave me not without offspring, though thou art the best of inheritors."

(90) So We listened to him: and We granted him Yahya [John]: We cured his wife's (barrenness) for him. These (three) were ever quick in emulation in good works; they used to call on Us with love and reverence, and humble themselves before Us.

(91) And (remember) her who guarded her chastity [Mary]: We breathed into her of Our spirit, and We made her and her son a sign for all peoples.

In the example below, "the poets" from Muhammad's context are challenged with the revelation to which he called people; the poets are called to consider the example of Abraham and his prayer in verses 83-89.[67]

Sura 26:69-89, The Poets (ash-Shu'ara')
(69) And rehearse to them (something of) Abraham's story.

(70) Behold, he said to his father and his people: "What worship ye?"

(71) They said: "We worship idols, and we remain constantly in attendance on them."

(72) He said: "Do they listen to you when ye call (on them)?"

(73) "Or do you good or harm?"

(74) They said: "Nay, but we found our fathers doing thus (what we do)."

(75) He said: "Do ye then see whom ye have been worshipping—

(76) "Ye and your fathers before you?"

(77) "For they are enemies to me; not so the Lord and Cherisher of the Worlds;

(78) "Who created me, and it is He Who guides me;

(79) "Who gives me food and drink,

(80) "And when I am ill, it is He Who cures me;

(81) "Who will cause me to die, and then to life (again);

(82) "And who, I hope, will forgive me my faults on the day of Judgment."

(83) "O my Lord! bestow wisdom on me, and join me with the righteous;

(84) "Grant me honourable mention on the tongue of truth among the latest (generations);

(85) "Make me one of the inheritors of the Garden of Bliss;

(86) "Forgive my father, for that he is among those astray;

(87) "And let me not be in disgrace on the Day when (men) will be raised up—

(88) "The Day whereon neither wealth nor sons will avail,

(89) "But only he (will prosper) that brings to Allah a sound heart. . . ."

Sura 27:62, The Ant (an-Naml)[68]

Or, Who listens to the (soul) distressed when it calls on Him, and Who relieves its suffering, and makes you (mankind) inheritors of the earth? (Can there be another) god besides Allah? Little it is that ye heed!

Sura 29:45, The Spider (al-'Ankabut)

Recite what is sent of the Book by inspiration to thee, and establish regular Prayer: for Prayer restrains from shameful and unjust deeds; and remembrance of Allah is the greatest (thing in life) without doubt. And Allah knows the (deeds) that ye do.

Here below, two more figures, also found in the Bible, are represented as having prayed to Allah for help and received it.

Sura 38:34-36, The Letter (Sad) (34)

And We did try Solomon: We placed on his throne a body (without life); but he did turn (to Us in true devotion):

(35) He said, "O my Lord! Forgive me, and grant me a kingdom which, (it may be), suits not another after me: for Thou art the Grantor of Bounties (without measure)."

(36) Then We subjected the wind to his power, to flow gently to his order, Whithersoever he willed . . .

(41) Commemorate Our Servant Job. Behold he cried to his Lord: "The Evil One has afflicted me with distress and suffering!"

(42) (The command was given:) "Strike with thy foot: here is (water) wherein to wash, cool and refreshing, and (water) to drink."

(43) And We gave him (back) his people, and doubled their number, as a Grace from Ourselves, and a thing for commemoration, for all who have Understanding.

Sura 40:65, The Forgiving One (al-Mu'min)

He is the Living (One): There is no god but He: Call upon Him, giving Him sincere devotion. Praise be to Allah, Lord of the Worlds!

The sura below attends to the obligatory Friday prayer and the expectation of its discipline, though human nature tends to become distracted.

Sura 62:9-11, Friday (al-Jumu'ah)

(9) O ye who believe! When the call is proclaimed to prayer on Friday (the Day of Assembly), hasten earnestly to the Remembrance of Allah, and leave off business (and traffic): That is best for you if ye but knew!

(10) And when the Prayer is finished, then may ye disperse through the land, and seek of the Bounty of Allah: and celebrate the Praises of Allah often (and without stint): that ye may prosper.

(11) But when they see some bargain or some amusement, they disperse headlong to it, and leave thee standing. Say: "The (blessing) from the Presence of Allah is better than any amusement or bargain! and Allah is the Best to provide (for all needs)."

Here again is a linkage shown between practice of prayer and compassion for those who are vulnerable.

Sura 107:1-7, Alsmgiving (al-Ma'un)

(1) Seest thou one who denies the Judgment (to come)?

(2) Then such is the (man) who repulses the orphan (with harshness),

(3) And encourages not the feeding of the indigent.

(4) So woe to the worshippers

(5) Who are neglectful of their prayers,

(6) Those who (want but) to be seen (of men),

(7) But refuse (to supply) (even) neighbourly needs.

The specific kind of prayer called *du'ā'* (supplication, or a calling upon Allah), which most precisely fits the lament prayer we have been discussing, is isolated out from twenty-five Qur'an verses, as below. About half of these are also confessional, seeking forgiveness. Besides the *du'ā'* in the Qur'an, such prayers can be made in any language and for countless needs. Muhammad taught how to pray a *du'ā'*.[69]

1.　Our Lord! Grant us good in this world and good in the life to come and keep us safe from the torment of the Fire. (2:201)

2.　Our Lord! Bestow on us endurance and make our foothold sure and give us help against those who reject faith. (2:250)

3.　Our Lord! Take us not to task if we forget or fall into error. (2:286)

4.　Our Lord! Lay not upon us such a burden as You did lay upon those before us. (2:286)

5.　Our Lord! Impose not on us that which we have not the strength to bear, grant us forgiveness and have mercy on us. You are our Protector. Help us against those who deny the truth. (2:286)

6. Our Lord! Let not our hearts deviate from the truth after You have guided us, and bestow upon us mercy from Your grace. Verily You are the Giver of bounties without measure. (3:8)

7. Our Lord! Forgive us our sins and the lack of moderation in our doings, and make firm our steps and succour us against those who deny the truth. (3:147)

8. Our Lord! Whomsoever You shall commit to the Fire, truly You have brought [him] to disgrace, and never will wrongdoers find any helpers. (3:192)

9. Our Lord! Behold we have heard a voice calling us unto faith: "Believe in your Lord" and we have believed. (3:193)

10. Our Lord! Forgive us our sins and efface our bad deeds and take our souls in the company of the righteous. (3:193)

11. Our Lord! And grant us that which you have promised to us by Your messengers and save us from shame on the Day of Judgement. Verily You never fail to fulfill Your promise. (3:194)

12. Our Lord! We have sinned against ourselves, and unless You grant us forgiveness and bestow Your mercy upon us, we shall most certainly be lost! (7:23)

13. Our Lord! Place us not among the people who have been guilty of evildoing. (7:47)

14. Our Lord! Lay open the truth between us and our people, for You are the best of all to lay open the truth. (7:89)

15. Our Lord! Pour out on us patience and constancy, and make us die as those who have surrendered themselves unto You. (7:126)

16. Our Lord! Make us not a trial for the evildoing folk, and save as by Your mercy from people who deny the truth. (10:85-86)

17. Our Lord! You truly know all that we may hide [in our hearts] as well as all that we bring into the open, for nothing whatever, be it on earth or in heaven, remains hidden from Allah. (14:38)

18. Our Lord! Bestow on us mercy from Your presence and dispose of our affairs for us in the right way. (18:10)

19. Our Lord! Grant that our spouses and our offspring be a comfort to our eyes, and give us the grace to lead those who are conscious of You. (25:74)

20. Our Lord! You embrace all things within Your Grace and Knowledge, forgive those who repent and follow Your path, and ward off from them the punishment of Hell. (40:7)

21. Our Lord! Make them enter the Garden of Eden which You have promised to them, and to the righteous from among their fathers, their wives and their offspring, for verily You are alone the Almighty and the truly Wise. (40:8)

22. Our Lord! Relieve us of the torment, for we do really believe. (44:12)

23. Our Lord! Forgive us our sins as well as those of our brethren who proceeded us in faith and let not our hearts entertain any unworthy thoughts or feelings against [any of] those who have believed. Our Lord! You are indeed full of kindness and Most Merciful. (59:10)

24. Our Lord! In You we have placed our trust, and to You do we turn in repentance, for unto You is the end of all journeys. (60:4)

25. Our Lord! Perfect our light for us and forgive us our sins, for verily You have power over all things. (66:8)

We have mentioned that there are many recognized reciters of the Qur'an, but perhaps one of the most influential and popular singers in the Arab world who composed some of her songs based on Qur'an texts was the late Umm Kulthūm of Egypt, widely beloved and revered.[70]

An early collection (seventh to eighth century C.E.), *The Psalms of Islam* (of the Household of Muhammad), revered especially by Shi'a but also by Sunni Muslims, contains prayers believed to have been composed largely by the fourth imam, 'Alī ibn al-Ḥusayn, known as Zayn Al-'Abidīn, great grandson of Muhammad. He himself was sorely acquainted with a depth of grief for many years over the death of his father, Imam Ḥusayn, and other family members. Here is an excerpt of a psalm by Zayn Al-'Abidīn, known as Supplication 13:

O God,
O ultimate object of needs!
O He through whom requests are attained!
O He whose favours are not bought by prices!
. . . O He toward whom desire is ever directed
and never turned away!
O He whose treasuries cannot be exhausted by demands!
O He whose wisdom cannot be altered by any means!
O He from whom the needs of the needy are never cut off!
O He who is not distressed by the supplications of the
    supplicators!

. . . O God,
bless Muhammed and his Household,
take me through Thy generosity to Thy gratuitous bounty
and take me not through Thy justice to what I deserve!
I am not the first beseecher to beseech Thee
and Thou bestowed upon him
while he deserved withholding. . . .

O God,
bless Muhammad and his Household,
respond to my supplication,
come near to my call,
have mercy on my pleading,
listen to my voice,
cut not short my hope for Thee,
sever not my thread to Thee,

turn not my face in this my need,
and other needs,
away from Thee. . . .

And of my needs, My Lord, are . . .
Thy bounty has comforted me
and Thy beneficence has shown the way,
So I ask Thee by Thee
and by Muhammad and his Household
(Thy blessings be upon them)
that Thou sendest me not back in disappointment! (lines 1-3,
    6-10, 20-22, 25)[71]

The custom of Shi'a mourning for Imam Ḥusayn has been mentioned; there are some analogies to the suffering and commemoration of Jesus' redemptive death.[72] It is beyond the scope of this
book, but the recitation or singing of laments from the sacred texts,
as well as other lament prayers, mourning rituals, and liturgies, continues in the Abrahamic faiths throughout history.[73]

———— ∞∞∞ ————

CHAPTER FIVE

Lament, the Prophetic Vision, and Social Justice

The Abrahamic faiths share an emphasis on the prophetic heritage and its concern for those who suffer and lament their oppression, poverty, or hardship.

Jeremiah

> Teach to your daughters a dirge, and each to her neighbor a lament. (Jer 9:20b)

The prophet Jeremiah was an important contributor to the lament tradition of the Hebrew Bible. He was called by God to an extraordinarily difficult, if not impossible, task (Jer 1:1-19). His prophetic responsibility was to convince the people of Judah (his own people) to change course, from a path of injustice and the idolatry of following a dangerous political alliance, to following and trusting YHWH alone and practicing Torah ethics. In a sense, the prophet was called upon, through judgment speeches to the people, *to lament God's lament*, or God's complaint against them. The biblical prophets often used legal terminology in bringing such a case. YHWH's complaint stemmed from divine compassion and anger, that the leaders and people were oppressing their own poor and vulnerable ones. In a sense, this was the prophet's "self-criticism" of his own people or nation. This aspect of the influential prophetic tradition is one of the extraordinary legacies of ancient Israel when compared with surrounding cultures. That an individual such as Jeremiah, who cared deeply for his own people, was called upon to make this criticism put him in an agonizing position, especially as he began to see the futility of his own efforts and the impending disaster that was about to befall. The destruction of Judah, Jerusalem, and the temple, the severe hardships imposed by the Babylonians, and the exile of the leaders first, then the majority of the people following in the early sixth century B.C.E., marked the most serious crisis in ancient Israel's history thus far. It was to mean the loss of the heritage of a homeland and a return to slavery.

This cauldron into which Jeremiah was called caused him to compose numerous personal laments, some of which we will consider below.[1] Previously I have proposed that the complex array of voices in the book of Jeremiah suggests that he was in dialogue with a woman lament singer, or perhaps a female prophet, and she may be the referent of his term of endearment, Bat-ʿammî ("daughter of my people").[2] This is suggested by this voice's direct speech (lyrics) in the text, "unmediated" and unintroduced by the prophet, but included by a scribe or redactor. These lyrics, in 4:19-21, 8:18, 10:19-20, and 10:22-25, have been identified by some as the voice of "Jerusalem/Daughter of Zion," the personified city, which is rendered by Jeremiah's poetry elsewhere. However, I proposed that the lyrical speeches were not simply the prophet's construction of a speaking persona, but were the lyrics of another poet/singer. I suggested that it is this poet's voice that also continues in dialogue with him into the book of Lamentations, along with at least two other voices. The lament poetry of the two voices was examined for consistency in their specific uses of genre, imagery, terminology, rhetorical technique, and thematic and theological content. Thus, I propose that in Lamentations, Jeremiah's voice is one among several lamenters, and that he is not the only "author" of the book, as tradition suggests by the book's attributing superscript.[3]

There is not enough space to treat fully all the lament texts of Jeremiah, but the examples to follow here will give an impression of Jeremiah's voice (as much as such a matter can be known), and something of the dynamic suggested between him and the other lament singer, as well as with the "mourning women" who sang dirges. We should be reminded that this was an oral traditional culture, and lament songs across cultures worldwide, as well as poetry in the Bible, display a dialogical performance style. This would be reflected even in the "literary" text written down for posterity and likely to have been edited by redactor(s) for the canon.

Recently, feminist and womanist commentators have helpfully critiqued the problem in the text of the misogynist metaphor for Jerusalem (and the people) as an unfaithful wife deserving abusive punishment. Unfortunately, Jeremiah's rhetoric participated in a larger prophetic tradition that employed such terminology to suggest the problematic covenant relationship with God. However, an excessive preoccupation with this rhetoric by commentators has at the same time overshadowed Jeremiah's empathy for the people, portrayed in the biblical book of the same name. Surely, he experienced a tension and inner turmoil about his task, including complaints to God about unacceptable divine harshness, which these very metaphors rendered. Finally, we will also consider some of God's laments, for God's controversy with the people, as the book of Jeremiah portrays, was not without divine grief over a very troubled relationship.

(Jeremiah, a lament/complaint against God)

Then I said, "Ah, LORD God, how utterly you have deceived
this people and Jerusalem, saying, 'It shall be well with you,'
even while the sword is at the throat!" (Jer 4:10)

(Lament singer)[4]

My viscera! my viscera! I labor in anguish!
The walls of my heart!
My heart is in turmoil;
I cannot keep silent;
for the sound of the shofar I hear—oh my soul!—

the alarm of battle.
The clamor of destruction upon destruction—
[crushing upon crushing]
indeed!—the whole land is devastated.
Suddenly my tents are devastated,
my curtains in a moment!
How long must I see the signal—
hear the sound of the shofar!? (Jer 4:19-21)

**(Jeremiah utters a cosmic dirge as warning, rendering the
creation coming undone)**

I look upon the earth, and behold!—"waste and void,"
and unto the heavens and there is no light!
I look to the mountains, and behold! they are quaking,
and all the hills shaking.
I look and behold! there is no "adam"!
and all the birds of the heavens flee.
I look and behold! the garden-land a desert!
and all its cities are pulled down,
on account of YHWH,
on account of his burning anger. (Jer 4:23-26)

(Lament singer)

My joy has gone; grief is upon me; my heart is faint. (Jer 8:18)

(Jeremiah)

Listen! A sound! A cry for help from Bat-ʻammî ["Daughter
of My People"], those being removed from the land. . . .
(Jer 8:19a)

(Jeremiah)

For the crushing of Bat-ʻammî
I am crushed; I mourn,
dismay has seized me.
Is there no balm in Gilead?

Is there no physician there?
Why is the wound of Bat-'ammî not healed? (Jer 8:21-22)

(Jeremiah)

O that my head were a spring of water,
and my eyes a fountain of tears,
that I might cry day and night
for the slain Bat-'ammî! (Jer 9:1)

(God)

O that I had in the desert a wayfarer's hut—
let me leave my people and go away from them! (Jer 9:2a)

The last two laments are interesting. Jeremiah laments for the suffering of Bat-'ammî (either a term of endearment for a person, perhaps the lament singer herself, or a symbolic name for the people), while God laments from displeasure with the people's behavior and wishes to leave the scene, to get away from them! Here is a divergence between the perspectives of God and God's prophet. I have isolated the dialogical exchange above between Jeremiah and the woman's lamenting voice. Interspersed as well in their dialogue in the larger text are God's repeated interjections of angry judgment.

A shift occurs in the flow at Jeremiah 9:17-22, when God calls for the mourning women to come and raise dirge songs over the communal destruction. God had previously prohibited any further lament prayer as being futile in the context (in 7:16, and later in 11:14, and 14:11). No more lament prayer, no more appeal to God, is to be accepted that might change the course of events. The text suggests that some women dutifully raise dirges, rather than lament prayers, but the woman lament singer who is previously heard is about to ignore God's request and pray a lament to God anyway.

(God)[5]

Thus says the LORD of hosts:
Consider, and call for the mourning women to come;

send for the skilled women to come;
let them quickly raise a dirge over us,
so that our eyes may run down with tears,
and our eyelids flow with water.
For a sound of wailing is heard from Zion:
"How we are ruined! We are utterly shamed,
because we have left the land,
because they have cast down our dwellings."
Hear, O women, the word of the LORD,
and let your ears receive the word of his mouth;
teach to your daughters a dirge, and each to her neighbor a
    lament.
"Death has come up into our windows,
it has entered our palaces,
to cut off the children from the streets
and the young men from the squares."
Speak! Thus says the LORD:
"Human corpses shall fall like dung upon the open field,
like sheaves behind the reaper, and no one shall gather them."
    (Jer 9:17-22)

The exchange between the lament singer and Jeremiah continues to unfold:

(Lament singer)[6]

Woe is me because of my crushing!
My wound gushes.
But I say, "Truly this is my piercing,
and I will bear it.
My tent is devastated
and all my cords are snapped;
my children have gone out from me,
and are no more.
There is no one any more to stretch out my tent,
or set my curtains." (Jer 10:19-20)

(Jeremiah)

How stupid are the shepherds!
because YHWH they did not seek;
they have not been prudent,
and all their flock is scattered!
—a sound is heard! listen! it is coming—
a great rumbling from the land of the north,
to make the cities of Judah a desolation,
a lair of jackals. (Jer 10:21-22)

(Lament singer; a confessional lament to God)

I know, YHWH,
    that the path of humans is not their own,
    and it is not for a man, as he walks, to direct his own steps.
Correct me, YHWH, but with justice,
    and not with your anger, lest you diminish/belittle me.
Pour out your wrath
    on the peoples that have not known you,
    and upon the clans that have not called on your name;
    for they have devoured Jacob;
    they have devoured him and consumed him,
    and have desolated his pasture-abode. (Jer 10:23-25)

It is interesting that after the lament singer finally offers a confessional lament prayer to God, soon thereafter Jeremiah begins a long series of his own personal laments to God. Here are a few examples:

(Jeremiah) [7]

It was the LORD who made it known to me, and I knew;
then you showed me their evil deeds.
But I was like a gentle lamb led to the slaughter.
And I did not know it was against me that they devised schemes,
saying, "Let us destroy the tree with its fruit,
let us cut him off from the land of the living,

so that his name will no longer be remembered!"
But you, O LORD of hosts, who judge righteously,
who try the heart and the mind,
let me see your retribution upon them,
for to you I have committed my cause. (Jer 11:18-20)

(Jeremiah)

You will be in the right, O LORD,
when I lay charges against you;
but let me put my case to you.
Why does the way of the guilty prosper?
Why do all who are treacherous thrive?
You plant them, and they take root;
they grow and bring forth fruit;
you are near in their mouths yet far from their hearts.
But you, O LORD, know me;
You see me and test me—my heart is with you.
Pull them out like sheep for the slaughter,
and set them apart for the day of slaughter.
How long will the land mourn,
and the grass of every field wither?
For the wickedness of those who live in it
the animals and the birds are swept away,
and because people said, "He is blind to our ways." (Jer 12:1-4)

(God's answer)

If you have raced with foot-runners and they have wearied you,
how will you compete with horses?
And if in a safe land you fall down,
how will you fare in the thickets of the Jordan?
For even your kinsfolk and your own family,
even they have dealt treacherously with you;
they are in full cry after you;
do not believe them,
though they speak friendly words to you. (Jer 12:5-6)

In another instance God directs Jeremiah to warn King Jehoiakim, who has been unfaithful and corrupt, that when he dies, there will be no dirge sung in his honor.

(God)

> Are you a king because you compete in cedar?
> Did not your father eat and drink
> and do justice and righteousness?
> Then it was well with him.
> He judged the cause of the poor and needy. . . .
> But your eyes and heart
> are only on your dishonest gain,
> for shedding innocent blood,
> and for practicing oppression and violence.
> Therefore thus says the LORD concerning King Jehoiakim
> son of Josiah of Judah:
> They shall not lament for him, saying,
> "Alas, my brother!" or "Alas, sister!"
> They shall not lament for him, saying,
> "Alas, lord!" or "Alas, his majesty!"
> With the burial of a donkey he
> shall be buried—
> dragged off and thrown out
> beyond the gates of Jerusalem. (Jer 22:15-19)

Finally, here is an example of God's lament of sorrow over Israel (figured in Rachel, mother in early Israel, and in one of the tribes, Ephraim). In each case, divine sorrow moves God to answer the people's lament. The people and covenant will be restored and made new (Jer 31:31).

(God)

> Thus says the LORD:
> A voice is heard in Ramah, lamentation and bitter weeping.
> Rachel is weeping for her children;
> she refuses to be comforted for her children,

because they are no more.
Thus says the LORD:
Keep your voice from weeping, and your eyes from tears;
for there is a reward for your work, says the LORD:
they shall come back from the land of the enemy;
there is hope for your future, says the LORD:
your children shall come back to their own country.
Indeed I heard Ephraim pleading:
"You disciplined me, and I took the discipline;
I was like a calf untrained. Bring me back, let me come back,
for you are the LORD my God.
For after I had turned away I repented . . .
I was ashamed, and I was dismayed
because I bore the disgrace of my youth."
Is Ephraim my dear son? Is he the child I delight in?
As often as I speak against him, I still remember him.
Therefore I am deeply moved for him;
I will surely have mercy on him, says the LORD. (Jer 31:15-20)

Historic and Contemporary Prophetic Lament

With the example of the woman lamenter and other mourners in
Jeremiah, we see what we have already seen across cultures worldwide and through history: the burden of this duty on women. Yet,
while women are often expected to lament, by way of a double
standard their voices are often ignored as unimportant or simply
emotional. The many examples of women's laments thus far suggest
the complete opposite. Lament is not mere wailing; it is heartfelt,
reasoned, poignant artistry, an important expression for questioning
and for human healing and wholeness. It is not surprising that the
prophet Jeremiah, at Israel's greatest ancient crisis, was in dialogue
with a woman lamenter. In the Jewish aggadot, the account of "the
Great Lament" by Mother Rachel (related to Jeremiah 31 above)
is what moved God to finally restore Judah (Israel) from Babylonian exile. Today, Rachel's Lament is read on the second day of
Rosh Hashanah in the Jewish community (in the *haftara*, or pro-

phetic reading, of Jer 31:1-19). There also developed historic and contemporary musical arrangements of Rachel's lament.[8]

From a recent Christian perspective on Jeremiah comes a lament warning of the impending war's destruction in her town of Mostar in 1992. Here we see the biblical lament pattern of many questions and no answer, and in this case, of a woman taking on the lonely task of being a prophetic voice.

Jeremianic Lamentations over Bosnia and Herzegovina

Marija Koprivnjak

My proud Bosnia,
Must you go the way of Slovenia and Croatia?
Does there not exist a hand in the world
that will stop your war-fire and destruction?
Is your way of the cross too long?
When will you stop bleeding?
What will become of your bloody wounds?
Who will heal the countless broken hearts?
Who will raise again the countless demolished houses,
sanctuaries, factories, bridges, and tunnels?
Before all these questions one is left mute.
One finds no answers.[9]

In Muslim tradition, it is well known that Muhammed the prophet addressed the suffering of the poor and oppressed in Mecca and was himself persecuted for it. It is worth noting that none of the primary sacred texts of the Abrahamic religions—Hebrew Bible, New Testament, or Qur'an—retains any dirge-like lament for the spiritual progenitor of the tradition, whether Moses, Jesus, or Muhammed. Yet the spiritual heirs of these figures have been inspired by their sacrificial lives for generations.

The importance of the death of Jesus in the example below is conveyed not in the rhetorical genre of song or poem, but as an address to a funeral gathering. Realities of near despair, and daring hope, permeated the speech of Archbishop Desmond Tutu to the suffering and grief-stricken people of South Africa in 1977, upon the brutal torture and murder of Steve Biko, the beloved, young anti-apartheid leader. Archbishop Tutu spoke at Biko's funeral to more than fifteen thousand people in King William's Town (it was then still seventeen years before the "new South Africa"). There is so much here illustrative of our focus that I quote his address at length:

> ... No, it must be a horrible nightmare and we will awake and find that really it is different—that Steve is alive even if it be in detention. But no, dear friends, he is dead and we are still numb with grief and groan with anguish. Oh God, where are you? Oh, God, do you really care? How can you let this happen to us?
>
> It all seems such a senseless waste of a wonderfully gifted person, struck down in the bloom of life, a youthful bloom that some wanted to see blighted. What can be the purpose of such wanton destruction? God, do you really love us? What must we do which we have not done, what must we say which we have not said a thousand times over, oh, for so many years—that all we want is what belongs to all God's children, what belongs as an inalienable right: a place in the sun in our own beloved mother country. Oh, God, how long can we go on? How long can we go on appealing for a more just ordering of society where we all, black and white together, count not because of some accident of birth or a biological irrelevance, where all of us, black and white, count because we are human persons, human persons created in your own image.
>
> In our grief and through our tears, we recall. Let us recall, my dear friends, that nearly two thousand years ago a young man was done to death and hung like a common criminal on a cross outside a city where they jeered at him and made fun of him. Let us recall how his followers were dejected and quite inconsolable in their grief. It all seemed so utterly meaningless, so utterly futile. This young man, God's own son, Jesus Christ, had come preaching the good news of God's love for all his children. He came seeing himself as one who fulfilled the glorious prophecy of Isaiah:
>
> > "The Spirit of the Lord is upon me; because the Lord hath anointed me to preach good tidings unto the meek; he hath sent me to bind up the brokenhearted, to proclaim liberty to the captives, and the opening of the

prison to them that are bound; to proclaim the acceptable year of the Lord, and the day of vengeance of our God; to comfort all that mourn; to appoint unto them that mourn in Zion, to give unto them beauty for ashes, the oil of joy for mourning, the garment of praise for the spirit of heaviness; that they might be called trees of righteousness, the planting of the Lord, that he might be glorified. And they shall build the old wastes, they shall raise up the former desolations, and they shall repair the waste cities, the desolations of many generations." (Isa 61:1-4)

. . . Jesus saw himself as the son, the great liberator, God himself, the God who had sided with a miserable, oppressed and disorganized group of slaves. And this God had taken their side against their oppressors—this great God of the Exodus, with power and might, with an outstretched arm he had led this group of slaves victoriously out of their slavery in Egypt to the freedom of the Promised Land. . . Yes, this was the good news Jesus came to proclaim—that God was the liberator, the one who set free the oppressed and the poor and exploited. . . . And his followers believed he would restore the kingdom again to Israel. He would set them free from being ruled by the Romans and give them back their political independence. They had placed their hopes on him. And look at him now. This young man in his thirties who had said, "I have come that all might have life and that they might have life in all its fullness," look at him, dead, and all our hopes, said his followers, lie shattered with his death.

The powers of darkness, of evil and of destruction had done their worst, they had killed the Lord of life himself. But that death was not the end. That death was the beginning of a glorious life, the resurrection life. . . . The grave could not hold captive such a gloriously free life. Jesus burst the very bonds of death and what had seemed like an ignominious defeat and complete meaninglessness was proved to be a splendid victory. . . . We too, like the disciples of Jesus, have been stunned by the death of another young man in his thirties. A young man completely dedicated to the pursuit of justice and righteousness, of peace and reconciliation. . . .

God called him to be the founder father of the black consciousness movement. . . . It is a movement by which God, through

Steve, sought to awaken in the black person a sense of his intrinsic value and worth as a child of God. . . . We have the quite inexplicable action of the authorities in stopping those coming to mourn at Steve's funeral. . . . I want to say, with all the circumspection and sense of responsibility that I can muster, that people can take only so much. . . .

Let us dedicate ourselves anew to the struggle for the liberation of our beloved land, South Africa. Let us all, black and white together, not be filled with despondency and despair. Let us blacks not be filled with hatred and bitterness. For all of us, black and white together, shall overcome, nay, indeed have already overcome.[10]

The eulogy is a kind of dirge in prose, a profound tribute, which also includes a number of lament prayer pleas with descriptions of distress and complaint. One can see how both forms, taken together, are incredibly important for a healing process and for providing hope and unity for the community to carry on. The repeated questions to God in the archbishop's prayer are very typical of the lament psalms, and the echo of the repeated question in the South African freedom song, "Senzeni Na," cited earlier, comes to mind. In this case, the lamenter does not ask "What have we done?" Rather, the lamenter asks "What more can we do that we haven't done!" and "Do you care for us? Where are you?" Yet his later affirmation—that God does care, is the God of the exodus, and that Jesus' death and resurrection have a purpose—coincides with lament element #3 above (expression of trust in the deity; remembrance of past saving actions). One can see the immense challenge for a leader in this position, who must help hold his people together by drawing on their spiritual resources when God seems absent, and the challenge to the people's confidence themselves. Add to this the archbishop's appeal that they not resort to hatred or violence in retaliation. That this is even possible, while surely a profound struggle, offers a great hope for humankind and a great example to the world. This is a departure from some of the biblical lament psalms in which the sufferer expresses the desire or feelings that God would avenge or punish the enemy. We will return to that element in chapter 7.

It becomes apparent that lament is associated with lone, "prophetic" type leaders who may be persecuted. The famous Indian poet Rabindranath Tagore wrote the following song for those striving for freedom in India. It inspired Mahatma Gandhi in his prophetic struggle and was one of his favorite songs; it was used by one of his spiritual successors in the movement, Vinoba Bhave.

Ekla Cholo Re ("Walk Alone")

Rabindranath Tagore

If they answer not to thy call walk alone,
If they are afraid and cower mutely facing the wall,
O thou of evil luck,
open thy mind and speak out alone.

If they turn away, and desert you when crossing the wilderness,
O thou of evil luck,
trample the thorns under thy tread,
and along the blood-lined track travel alone.

If they do not hold up the light when the night
    is troubled with storm,
O thou of evil luck,
with the thunder flame of pain ignite thy own heart
and let it burn alone.[11]

Voices around the world are calling out for the just treatment and release of Aung San Suu Kyi of Burma, detained in isolation under house arrest by the Myanmar regime for much of the last twenty years. She and the dissidents in Burma, including the Buddhist nuns, monks, and people of other faiths or of secular persuasion, are threatened with reprisal if they speak out.

In The Quiet Land

Daw Aung San Suu Kyi

In the Quiet Land, no one can tell
if there's someone who's listening

for secrets they can sell.
The informers are paid in the blood of the land
and no one dares speak what the tyrants won't stand.

In the quiet land of Burma,
no one laughs and no one thinks out loud.
In the quiet land of Burma,
you can hear it in the silence of the crowd.

In the Quiet Land, no one can say
when the soldiers are coming
to carry them away.
The Chinese want a road; the French want the oil;
the Thais take the timber; and SLORC[12] takes the spoils. . . .

In the Quiet Land . . .
In the Quiet Land, no one can hear
what is silenced by murder
and covered up with fear.
But, despite what is forced, freedom's a sound
that liars can't fake and no shouting can drown. [13]

CHAPTER SIX

Laments of the People

It is apparent in the books of Jeremiah, Lamentations, and Job that there is a struggle as to whether death and the dirge are to have the final say—whether lament prayer is of no use any more—or whether a persistent people shall yet lament in prayer to God as, and after, destruction has passed.[1] These books have been turned to by some for help in processing the great pain and losses of the Shoah, the post-Holocaust struggle, and other historical catastrophes.[2]

Biblical Lamentations

> Remember, O LORD, what has befallen us; look, and see
> our disgrace! (Lam 5:1)

Lament for an entire community or people, as well as lament by and for an individual, is attested across cultures and religious traditions. The biblical book of Lamentations[3] is many things: the graphic yet summative sorrow songs about the destruction of Judah and the temple, and the exile of the Judean people to Babylon in the sixth century B.C.E., the most devastating historic crisis before the Shoah; the expression and processing of pain;[4] the outcome of prophetic warnings, from Jeremiah and others, of God's punishment for the leaders' and people's wrongs and injustices; a wrangling of voices (including, it seems, a distraught Jeremiah and a woman lament singer/prophet in dialogue) and searing lament against God for the innocent sufferers, including children; an answering didactic voice about who is to blame, which pushes retributive justice ideology in defense of God; and in the end, five chapters of laments that go unanswered by God. The woman's voice, long neglected by commentators, has finally been attended to in recent years. That her voice goes beyond women's traditional mourning of dirge-singing to lead a dialogical debate about God's justice in the context is a striking challenge to the tradition's then-current theologies and acceptable gender roles.

Through the generations, Lamentations and its midrash have been read, along with Jeremiah and Job texts, as the basis for the Jewish Tishah B'Av service, which includes mourning practices for commemorating the destruction of the First and Second Temples, and the expulsion of Jews from Spain.[5] The songs of biblical Lamentations were probably composed in the midst and aftermath of the siege and destruction of Jerusalem in 587 B.C.E. Traditionally, in mourning contexts, singers composed by drawing upon and modifying stock lyrics and genres from the living oral tradition, improvising with thought, emotion, and inspiration to create new songs addressed to the immediate context. It is apparent that the singers drew on the lament traditions of the prophets and the psalms, yet the crisis was so extreme and complete that they pushed the genres to the utmost limits. In Lamentations, two lead singers are in dialogue; one comforts the other, a mourner, but they also modify traditional dirges and lament prayers strikingly in an intense interchange about suffering and justice.

The concerns of Lamentations for justice are evident in the two genres that the singers use to express their grief and to grapple with what has happened: the communal dirge (Lam 1, 2, and 4) and the lament prayer to God (parts of Lam 1, 2, 3, and all of 5). The communal dirge was typically uttered by Hebrew prophets as a warning to a community that both idolatry and social injustice will lead to its social collapse, the "death" of the nation. This genre, which opens Lamentations 1, reveals a prophetic point of view, describing disaster now after the fact, and is consistent with Jeremiah's lyricism, inasmuch as the individual artistry in this singer's songs closely parallels Jeremiah's poetry in the book of Jeremiah.

> How alone she sits,
> the city once full of people;
> she has become like a widow;
> once great among the nations,
> "Princess among the provinces,"
> she has become a slave.
>
> She weeps and weeps in the night,
> with her tears on her cheeks;
> she has no one comforting her
> among all her lovers.
> All her friends have betrayed her;
> they have become her enemies. (Lam 1:1-2)[6]

After many lyrics describing Jerusalem's distress, the lament singer (presumably female, as she speaks of her motherhood and children) breaks in with a lament outcry to God:

> See—YHWH—my suffering/violation!
> How the enemy gloats! (Lam 1:9c)

In a call-and-response pattern, the first singer resumes his description of distress, and she breaks in along the way with more lament, throughout chapters 1 and 2. The first singer shows an increasingly compassionate engagement with the lamenter, even encouraging her to cry out to God. She audaciously calls God to task for not intervening to prevent the suffering of babies and children. She and the prophetic singer gradually join voices in expressing how God has destroyed them, as if the divine were an enemy. They unite in a growing complaint, in spite of the sins of the people for which the disaster has been interpreted as corporate punishment. The "tenor" of the lament singer's voice is in the spirit of Moses' complaints and matched in its severity only by the later complaints in Job.

Other voices join in the wrangling in chapter 3, and by the final lament in chapter 5, there is a "we" communal lament prayer song to YHWH. Their final lines, and indeed all of their laments in this text, ultimately go unanswered by God, and there is certainly no typical shift to praise and thanks to God. As Tod Linafelt aptly says, finally "the flicker of praise is extinguished in the final three verses"; his translation leaves the lament to trail off unresolved:[7]

> You, O LORD, will reign forever,
> enthroned from generation to generation.
> Why have you forgotten us utterly,
> forsaken us for so long?
> Take us back, LORD, to yourself, and we will come back.
> Renew our days as of old.
> For if truly you have rejected us,
> bitterly enraged against us. . . . (Lam 5:19-22)

Commentators have noted how there is consolation from God offered in Jeremiah 31, and also in the latter chapters of the book of Isaiah, from a prophet who offers God's comfort to the people in exile. But more recent commentators and those who have experienced the severest of traumas note the realism implied by the book of Lamentations, and the deeply felt absence of God. They resist an easy imposition of hope where it was lacking.

Through their daring lament being allowed to stand alongside the silence of God, the two singers implicitly begin to critique a strict theology of retributive justice, in which the wicked or unrighteous are punished and God hears, rescues, and rewards only the good or righteous—which, after all, is not the case. They also lay the groundwork for undermining a wider theological claim (also common in the ancient Near East) that the deity literally or simply leads a war to defeat a nation. The book's struggle with theodicy—how can a "just" God allow this suffering of the innocent?—foreshadows and likely influences a similar debate in Job and is relevant to later historical and post-Holocaust discussions of the presence/absence of God in the sufferings of the Jewish people.

Historic and Contemporary Laments of the People

William Morrow has shown how the biblical lament tradition was used by Jews attacked during the Crusades by Christians.[8] Jews were forced to convert or face death; tragically, most became martyrs, and family suicides were common. Morrow notes that the Ashkenazi synagogue liturgies preserved Isaac bar Shalom's poem "There is No One Like You among the Dumb" (dated 1147 C.E.) as a *zulat*, a supplementary poem inserted between standard prayers, to commemorate the destruction of Jewish communities in the Rhineland. The title reveals the poem's severe complaint against God, much like the poetry in Lamentations and Job. It suggests that God was being mute in the face of dire suffering, and there are echoes of God's absence when the Romans destroyed the Jerusalem temple. The medieval poem alludes to specific fragments of psalm laments, and some invert praise of God (as Job does) to reflect the people's horrible experience and sense of abandonment. Through the centuries, it was a practice of the living oral tradition of synagogue services that thousands of poetic *piyyuṭim*, with a variety of content besides this focus, were composed and added in order to embellish the liturgy. Morrow shows that claims that Jewish postbiblical lament ceased are not true, although the subsequent lament tradition was not as strong as in biblical times. Here is an excerpt of this poignant poem:

There Is No One Like You Among the Dumb

Isaac bar Shalom

There is no one like you among the dumb,
silent and passive towards those who create trouble!
Our many enemies are rising up.
When they meet together to revile us,
"Where is your king?" they insult us.
We have not backslidden nor acted treasonably.
Do not keep silence! (lines 1–7)

. . . they bound the children and their mothers
and burnt their skins by fire . . .
Do not keep silence! (lines 37–38, 42)

It was a crowded, charred pile
like an oven neither covered nor swept.
And the whole house of Israel wept at the burning.
Those falling into the flaming sparks of the LORD
were assigned the place of the exiles,
Hananiah, Mishael and Azariah.
Do not keep silence! (lines 43–49)

They treated the Torah of Moses as dung,
also the Talmud of Rabina and Rab Ashai.
Will you restrain yourself and keep silence at this?
Pages and parchments went to the swords,
and holy letters went flying—
divine writing engraved on the tablets!
Do not keep silence! (lines 50–56)

. . . Take ownership again of our remnants.
Let us look publicly on your miracles.
Ordain peace for us.
Our Holy One, show mercy on your scattered ones.
May a generous spirit support us.
Rise up, O our help, and redeem us.
Do not keep silence! (lines 85–91)[9]

Armenian poet Siamanto wrote "The Dance," about a massacre of Armenians by Turkish forces in Adana in southern Turkey in 1909, in what became a prologue to the Armenian genocide of 1915 carried out by the Ottoman Turkish government. The poet was executed by the government. Here is an excerpt from the poem:

The Dance

Siamanto

In the town of Bardez where Armenians
were still dying,
A German woman, trying not to cry
told me the horror she witnessed.

"This incomprehensible thing I'm telling you about,
I saw with my own eyes.
Behind my window of hell
I clenched my teeth
and watched with my pitiless eyes:
the town of Bardez turned
into a heap of ashes.
Corpses piled high as trees.
From the waters, from the springs,
from the streams and the road,
the stubborn murmur of your blood
still revenges in my ear. . . ."[10]

The Yiddish song "Our Town is Burning," about the destruction of the town of Przytyk in Poland, became a Jewish resistance song against the Nazis from the Kraków Ghetto. The reader can listen to a performance on the website of the U.S. Holocaust Memorial Museum.

Our Town is Burning

Mordecai Gebirtig

It's burning, brothers! It's burning!
Oh, our poor village, brothers, burns!
Evil winds, full of anger,
Rage and ravage, smash and shatter;
Stronger now that wild flames grow—
All around now burns!
And you stand there looking on
With futile, folded arms
And you stand there looking on—
While our village burns!

It's burning, brothers! It's burning!
Oh, our poor village, brothers, burns!
Soon the rabid tongues of fire
Will consume each house entire,
As the wild wind blows and howls—

The whole town's up in flames!
And you stand there looking on
With futile, folded arms,
And you stand there looking on—
While our village burns!

It's burning, brothers! Our town is burning!
Oh, God forbid the moment should arrive,
That our town, with us, together,
Should go up in ash and fire,
Leaving when the slaughter's ended
Charred and empty walls!
And you stand there looking on
With futile, folded arms,
And you stand there looking on—
While our village burns!

It's burning, brothers! Our town is burning!
And our salvation hangs on you alone.
If our town is dear to you,
Grab the buckets, douse the fire!
Show that you know how!
Don't stand there, brothers, looking on
With futile, folded arms,
Don't stand there, brothers, douse the fire!—
Our poor village burns![11]

Jewish poet A. L. Strauss, at the close of his Shoah-related poem,
"Lament for the European Exile," managed to write:

> . . . Can I mourn?
> I am an elegy . . .
> I will mourn and rise. . . . [12]

In its graphic descriptions of Jerusalem's destruction and the
resulting mass human suffering, the book of Lamentations shows
similarities to contemporary lament poems or outcries of attacked

peoples and destroyed communities around the world. Here are a few examples, most of which spend many lines describing the distress and devastation. Perhaps the only comfort is that many others around the world have experienced a similar catastrophe, and so there is some mutual understanding and empathy. However, there is also complaint about how so many in the world, and in one's own country, simply stand by and do nothing. In Lamentations 1:12a, the female lament singer cries out, "Is it nothing to you, all you who pass by? Look! and see if there is any pain like my pain!" With similar language, Archbishop Desmond Tutu voices the same plea when describing the apartheid police practices of stripping and body-searching people at roadblocks:

> Your dignity is not just rubbed in the dust. It is trodden underfoot and spat on. Our people are being killed as if they were but flies. *Is that nothing to you who pass by?* What must we say that we have not said? "God, give us eloquence such that the world will hear that all we want is to be recognized for what we are—human beings created in your image." *Is it nothing to the world* that 800 black pupils are arrested, some as young as seven, and have to spend the night in jail? Aren't you appalled and outraged? Would the West be so passive if the casualties were white rather than black?[13]

Muslims facing genocide in Sarajevo in the 1990s were helped and supported by sympathetic, courageous neighbors, including Christians, as well as by the Jewish community there who had gone through such trauma in World War II in the former Yugoslavia. In the poem cited earlier, "Record of the City in Blank Verse," the poet Ljubica Ostojić personifies the devastated city of Sarajevo, just as the authors of Lamentations personified Jerusalem. Ostojić wrote in the preface to her poems:

> Every night I have a dream that I re-build and heal the wounds of the destroyed cities. And then, they are the same again, as at the times before the infernal powers and human madness and misery came. They are familiar and eternal. But the City in which I lived this hell sticks to my own being. And our pain and deterioration

became the same. Will our wounds and ruins ever heal into scars?
. . . God Almighty alone knows that.[14]

Similarly, poet and scholar Borislav Arapović, who is a Croatian
from Bosnia-Herzegovina, spent time in devastated areas during the
wars of the early 1990s. While in Osijek, he wrote a desperate plea
that rather directly reflected his experience of a city under siege. His
complaint was that he could not get through to the outside world
that was preoccupied with its own business. Here is an excerpt:

Telefax from Croatia

hurriedly frenetically leafing searching turning
....
...99472.......99396........993170.......99422.... . . .
...dialing...oslo..rome......the hague.....prague.....
...budapest.....bucharest...brussels......vienna.....
    bern..........berlin.........bonn..........and all.....
...the baals.and.gods of this world....................
....
not a sound—no connection

oh God in Heaven
is there a fax anywhere
from madrid to moscow
that is not blocked by traders' quotes
assailed by lies of our killers
that could receive the message
from a shelter full of dread
from a deathly-silent classroom

osijek croatia september 17 1991[15]
Borislav Arapović

The genocides in Bosnia-Herzegovina and in Rwanda both happened in the early 1990s. Suzanne Nyiranyamibwa of Rwanda composed a song to describe the devastation to her people:

Lament of Victims of Genocide

Suzanne Nyiranyamibwa

I arrive in Rwanda. I lose all sense of direction
It's as if my heart has broken free and my body is drained
While my chest is filled with strange sensations
Wild grass has hidden the county paths
The beautiful hills of yesteryear are covered in ruins
There where children frolicked and played
Are places where vultures now roam
The tears of orphans give you no relief from pain
Mothers have had their children ripped from their breasts
Too many widows trapped between life and death

Chorus:
Ahhhhhh . . . How am I to manage? What am I to do? Who
    should I speak to?
Because even he who I might have spoken to exists no longer!

The churches of God are carpeted in dead bodies
Mines have been hidden to kill here and there
You are alive at sunrise but will you be so when it sets?
They herded human beings like troops of cattle
They drove the condemned to their fate

"To be a Tutsi they said was a crime for which death was the
    only suitable
punishment. The Hutu that refuses to kill is not worthy of life.
    As an
accomplice he must also die."

Of his family only a handful of unfortunates remain
They had appalling fun at their expense
They stripped them where they lived in broad daylight
The path to the place of execution was just like Golgotha
They mutilated them atrociously
    without fear of reprisal or remorse

Proudly boasting of their skills
Those that escaped the machetes were clubbed to death
"If you want to be shot you have to buy the bullet first"
And if you have not enough to bribe your way to freedom
Your only choice is to be hacked to death
The reality of the abomination was worse
    than the most accursed prophesies.

Their master plan was the eradication of a race
Your mother was wrong to bring you into the world
Even the innocent smiles of our babies didn't soften their hearts
I implored heaven that I would wake and all could be revealed
As a nightmare, but in vain
All remained implacable reality
As I didn't know what to do with my tears
I silently swallowed them

Our people are now in the hands of Imana[16]
Save us from desperation for it is unhealthy
Together let's fight hate and triumph over misery.[17]

Unspeakable horrors came raining down on the United States on September 11, 2001. For many in the United States, Bruce Springsteen's song "My City of Ruins" became their lament, and poignantly rendered the sufferings of 9/11, though the song was composed, one might say prophetically, before the disaster, to describe a city suffering from the effects of poverty. The power of music and lyrics, however, is to render meaning for new and changing contexts. Thus, his plaintive "rise up!" became an address to a beloved personified fallen city, much as the biblical singers sang passionately to devastated, fallen Jerusalem. His plea, rise up, expressed compassion for a brother fallen to his knees. The refrain suggested a bold cry of desperation and prayer to God to rise up and help. The chorus of two simple words might mean all these things, as well as an additional hidden imperative: Rise up! people, to the aid of those desperately needing help. Rise up! in resistance to wrong.

My City of Ruins

Bruce Springsteen

There's a blood red circle
On the cold dark ground
And the rain is falling down
The church door's thrown open
I can hear the organ's song
But the congregation's gone
My city of ruins
My city of ruins

Now the sweet bells of mercy
Drift through the evening trees
Young men on the corner
Like scattered leaves
The boarded up windows
The empty streets
While my brother's down on his knees
My city of ruins
My city of ruins

Come on, rise up!
Come on, rise up! . . .

Now with these hands
With these hands, with these hands
With these hands, I pray Lord
With these hands, with these hands
I pray for the strength, Lord . . .
I pray for your love, Lord . . .

Come on, rise up!
Come on, rise up![18]

Clyde Fant, a native of Louisiana, recently found solace and a means to lament New Orleans's suffering after Hurricane Katrina by using the model of biblical lamentations. His poem appeared first not in a newspaper, journal, or book, but on the Internet. It is a creative recomposing of Lamentations. As that ancient lament was seemingly infused with a prophetic voice sympathetic to the people, so the poet, in this excerpt, is compelled to question who was to blame for the suffering, especially for the unprotected innocents.

A Lament for New Orleans

Clyde Fant

How like a widow sits the city once so beautiful!
She weeps bitterly in the night, with tears on her cheeks,
Because there is none to comfort her.
She stretched forth her hands, but none came to her;
They heard how she was groaning, but none came unto her.
In her streets the flood bereaves;
In the sodden houses it is like death.
The leaders and elders of the city have fled,
but the poor are trapped within her levees.

Her friends have dealt treacherously with her;
Those who promised to help are worse than her enemies.
When she cried aloud, none came;
Smooth words promised much,
But they were empty rhetoric,
wells without water, phantom bread.
Shame! Shame upon us all . . .

Weep, weep for the great city!
Orators of platitudes, politicians of promises,
it is you who betrayed her!
You . . . neglected her when she reached out to you.
You channeled her rivers and harnessed her waters,
but for yourselves!
For the profits of your friends!
You caused her marshes to dry
and her wilderness to recede;
you brought the might of the waves

and the winds to her very doors.
The poor, those who dwelt in the lowest places,
who lived in miserable shanties of wood,
termite-ridden and forlorn,
Where none but the hopeless would dwell:
You have murdered them,
and their corpses drift in the brackish floods,
But their cries have gone up to God! [19]

Homeless Exiles

Devastations such as the above create massive numbers of exiles and displaced persons. Those persons compose laments about their experience, as the following examples show.

Ladysmith Black Mambazo, the South African singing group, performed "Homeless," suggestive of the many black men who were forced to the "homelands" to work, separated from their families for extended periods of time under the harshest conditions:

Homeless

Ladysmith Black Mambazo

Homeless, homeless . . .
Somebody cry why, why, why?[20]

In the millennia-long Jewish diaspora, millions in exile longed for the homeland, as is suggested in this poem by Rachel, well-known poet of Israel from Russia.

To my Country

Rachel

I have not sung you, my country,
not brought glory to your name
with the great deeds of a hero
or the spoils a battle yields.
But on the shores of the Jordan
my hands have planted a tree,

and my feet have made a pathway
through your fields.

Modest are the gifts I bring you.
I know this, mother.
Modest, I know, the offerings
of your daughter:
Only an outburst of song
on a day when the light flares up,
only a silent tear
for your poverty.[21]

Mahmoud Darwish, the late well-known Palestinian poet, wrote many laments about his homeland.

I Belong There

Mahmoud Darwish

I belong there. I have many memories. I was born as everyone is
    born.
I have a mother, a house with many windows, brothers, friends,
    and a prison cell with a chilly window!
I have a wave snatched by seagulls, a panorama of my own.
I have a saturated meadow. In the deep horizon of my word,
    I have a moon,
a bird's sustenance, and an immortal olive tree.
I have lived on the land long before swords
    turned man into prey.
I belong there. When heaven mourns for her mother, I return
    heaven to her mother.
And I cry so that a returning cloud might carry my tears.
To break the rules, I have learned all the words needed
    for a trial by blood.
I have learned and dismantled all the words in order to draw
    from them a single word: Home[22]

A song of Jamal Khambar, a Kurdish Iraqi, lamented the suffering and loss of his homeland:

There was nobody to cry . . .
I was as lost as a child in the bosom of the universe . . .
At the last moment, the flute started to speak. . . . [23]

Lami'ah Abbas Amarah laments the loss of life as it was in Iraq.

Tears on a Sad Iraqi Face

Lami'ah Abbas Amarah

I rested my head on an Iraqi chest and wept
his heart endured the same sorrow as mine
he caressed and calmed me; I slept.
as branches of sadness, interlaced between
our souls, moan even in our silence
O wailing heart, O most beautiful eyes
I have ever seen
what has united us?
the cruelty of this war?
Or the passion of love?

O sad face from my homeland.
what tears what love can wash that sad face?
O my family, now only terror fills their hunger,
fills their thirst. O the panic of resurrection.
Is there any road that does not lead
them to destruction and Hell.
Any shelter for them?
what age do we live in? an age of barbarism?
or an age of civilization,
disgraced by its deeds in Amiriyyah.

This is the gloom of a defeated knight,
his hands paralyzed,
his forehead bearing the brunt of destruction,
all the sadness of the burning palm trees
all the wailing songs from the South,
all the echoes of lamentation

o palm trees of Samawah
how much cruelty can exist in this world?
seventy thousand children, sweet as dates

—no, even sweeter—have fallen,
along with your burning leaves, for what sins O palm trees of
    Samawah?

Like a headstrong mare I was.
I tripped not
nor was I easy to subdue
possessing the pride of the palm trees,
of my homeland's ageless hospitality.

My pride was to starve, rather than to bend, defiant, like the
    palmtree.
Alas! Led I was one day to forget my pride
when my own guide misled me

Lo and behold! now I stretched out my hands asking for
    charities,
dispensed by the same hands which destroyed civilization.[24]

Sometimes, people of different faiths join together. Today, a lament
prayer song (in four languages) is offered up for the Sudanese
people, still languishing from genocide,[25] composed together by
Sudanese hip-hop artist Emmanuel Jal (one of the "lost boys"), a
Christian, along with traditional Sudanese musician Abdel Gadir
Salim, a Muslim.

Gua ("Peace," in Nuer)

Emmanuel Jal and Abdel Gadis Salim

Chorus (in Dinka and Nuer)
Teth loida nangua shegua keo bi Sudan shuop
Keo bi Sudan shuop An bi pio miet apey
Na bi koech ru thuk panda
Na bi koech ru leou panda

Chorus (English translation)
I will be so happy when there's peace in Sudan
When people come back to Sudan,
    my heart will be filled with joy
When people can go back home
When people will be able to support themselves
    in their homeland

Verse one (in Arabic, Nuer, Dinka, English)
Kede steni steni ni faker faker café baled lo
Can fi salam kede ganu genu ni salu salu
Farah kabir a yekuon fi Sudan
Yarobi asma coraktana yarobi asma salatana
Dare gua dare gua thil madefarkje
Eke shangode oh teh mal thorah keoh thil ramah
De nyuman nyo ke mai ke match kah thil ramah
De yande nyokah mai kah thil ramah deh mai
Door ke boeth en nomomo thil ma de farke keo
Deh nah lui thoran kah denah thoran tath thil ma
De parkeja I can't wait for that day an leu
Bi piu miat eret lo bi koech ro pink pandid e sudan

Verse one (English translation)
Oh wait, wait, let's think
Think how it would be
If there was peace in Sudan
Let's sing. Sing: "Oh my Lord
Hear our prayer, hear our prayer"
It will be so good when there'll be peace
In my homeland Sudan
Not one sister will be forced into marriage
And not one cow will be taken by force
And not one person will starve from hunger again
I can't compare to anything
The time when people will understand each other
And there's peace in my homeland, Sudan

Verse two (originally in English)
Just hold on a minute, think for a minute
How it will be if there is peace in Sudan?
Our hands will be raised, our God will be praised
When my people will plant seed in their land
When my people will be free in their land
Ya ya, ya ya, I can't, I can't wait for that day
When I will see no more tears, no more fear, no cry
No tribalism, nepotism and racism in my motherland
I can't wait for that day when
    the wonderful people go back home
And plan their nation in this generation
I can't wait to see that day

Verse three (in Nuer)
Jen waidah mah she shuop deh loidah teth
Elong keo guaa mah sheakenommo
Bi ngane ngach ah bi ouh thil leah kah
Bi hou thil bouch en wano bane uh lat nah
Waidan ke tet kel ke loch kel ke puony
Kel ke riem kel kah wano bah kon luoth
A weitah oh kian Sudanese bane kel keoh
De gat kon guar e wano e kon neitah gow I hope we can do this

Verse three (English translation)
When there will be peace I will be truly happy
At that moment there will be no more death
No more hunger and we shall rebuild our land
The whole world will respect us
And we shall rebuild our land
With one hand, one heart, with one blood, one body
Because we are one
And Sudan's future shall be promising
Children will go to school, I hope we can do this.[26]

And now, the people of the Democratic Republic of the Congo have been victimized by a civil war and genocidal killings, with individuals from Rwanda who perpetrated genocide there also having come to the Congo. The organization Genocide Watch has issued a "genocide alert" for the country, stating that all eight stages of a genocidal process are unfolding there, and calling for the international community's intervention. Over the last ten years, it is estimated that four to five million Congolese have lost their lives, and current living conditions are desperate.[27]

PART THREE

Lament for Our Time

⁂

CHAPTER SEVEN

Developing Constructive Lament: Mourning and Nonviolent Justice

W hile this book has not dwelled on it, the problem of violence and revenge can be implicit or explicit in some expressions of lament across cultures and religions. Yet the problematic linkage between religion and violence or revenge was not created by Jews, Christians, or Muslims. These areas already intersected in ancient Near Eastern and other traditional cultures.[1]

Violence, Revenge, Weariness, and Innovating Genres

Dirge forms across cultures could include a "call for vengeance," reflecting social custom, if a death was caused by injustice.[2] At the same time, adherents of all of the Abrahamic faiths have obviously carried out violence at certain points in history. On the other hand, they each have within their traditions the seeds and the potential for a higher, nonviolent path.

In the Hebrew Bible

A number of lament psalms move, toward their end, with the lamenter calling for God to bring vengeance or punishment against the enemy. Psalm 140 will suffice as one example:

> Deliver me, O LORD, from evildoers;
> protect me from those who are violent. . . .
> Those who surround me lift up their heads;
> let the mischief of their lips overwhelm them!
> Let burning coals fall on them!
> Let them be flung into pits, no more to rise! (Ps 140:1, 9-10)

A defense for the inclusion of this call for violent punishment might be that at least the psalm (as a prayer) allows the lamenter to vent human feelings, to necessarily cry out an injustice, to be heard, and to turn such desires over to God, who has the power to transform and cleanse the lamenter of destructive feelings and forces. All this rather than the lamenter carrying out an action of vengeance himself or herself. Bringing the lament before the faith community means also bringing it into the sphere of other operative principles and realities—of God's ultimate control over judgment and punishment, of practices of love, justice, forgiveness, and reconciliation—which might serve to curb the lamenter's need to exact violent vengeance. On the other hand, it might be argued (and lectionary editors seem to follow this line of thinking) that the mere articulating of the desire for vengeful violence may trigger the human carrying out of retribution by the lamenter's fellow community members on his or her behalf. Such texts can be dangerous, can be taken out of context, exploited or manipulated to sanction sociopolitical violence that leaders or peoples might take against their enemies. Lectionary compilers and liturgists have taken measures either to avoid such texts or to edit them. One problem is that there is not always full understanding of the positive contribution to faith of the lament genre, so that often mere protest or complaints against God are completely removed, as being too negative. Communities will decide about this, but many people need a liturgical way to process feelings of suffering, sorrow, and even abandonment in their time of crisis. The alternative is to so edit the Scripture as to render a faith that denies the full range of human experience and that becomes irrelevant to those who sorely suffer.

In the New Testament

The New Testament includes rhetoric of severe conflict between Jesus and his followers and other Jews, as well as passages that describe the end-time as being the moment when Christ returns as violent warrior to conquer the enemies of God. One example will suffice:

> Then I saw heaven opened, and there was a white horse!
> Its rider is called Faithful and True, and in righteousness
> he judges and makes war. His eyes are like a flame of fire . . .
> He is clothed in a robe dipped in blood,
> and his name is called The Word of God . . .
> From his mouth comes a sharp sword with which
> to strike down the nations, and he will rule them with a rod of
> iron. . . . (Rev 19:11-15)

In the Qur'an

Texts that seem to condone battle against nonbelievers are dangerous for potentially leading to violence. Here is one example:

> Once the sacred months have passed,
> you may kill the idolaters when you encounter them,
> and take them [captive], and besiege them,
> and prepare for them each ambush.
> But if they repent and establish worship and pay the poor-due,
> then leave their way free. Lo! God is Forgiving, Merciful.
>   (Surah 9:5)

These verses come from a context when early Muslims were attacked by military aggressors and granted a right to defend themselves.[3] At the same time, this and the above examples have dangerous potential because irresponsible readers may exploit them to support political violence and the oppression of others.

Beyond our sacred texts, there is the sense that people around the world are weary with massively destructive forces and old ways, as reflected in the following poems.

Blackout

Ittamir Yaoz-Kest

Blindly from the window
the woman stares at the street.
They are piling sandbags.

Over the glass
she sticks paper strips:
war over war. Her sudden reflection

appears in the panes, a crowd
of faces. Tired, she listens
for a long time to the shuddering

echo of boots on the stairs,
army boots moving up and down
and up again

like blood pressure, and she doesn't
know if it's now
or years before.[4]

A long journey together with lament leads us to some important destinations of sober realization. First, children and youth are by and large the greatest victims in a world in which lament continues to describe our tragic human condition.

Written in Pencil in the Sealed Railway-Car

Dan Pagis

here in this carload
I am eve
with abel my son[5]

The Artist Child

Dunya Mikhail

—I want to draw the sky.
—Draw it, my darling.
—I have.
—And why do you spread
the colors this way?
—Because the sky has no edges.
. . .
—I want to draw the earth.
—Draw it, my darling.
—I have.
—And who is this?
—She is my friend.
—And where is the earth?
—In her handbag.
. . .
—I want to draw the moon.
—Draw it, my darling.
—I can't.
—Why?
—The waves shatter it
continuously.
. . .
—I want to draw paradise.
—Draw it, my darling.
—I have.
—But I don't see any colors.
—It is colorless.
. . .
—I want to draw the war.
—Draw it, my darling.
—I have.
—And what is this circle?
—Guess.
—A drop of blood?

—No.
—A bullet?
—No.
—Then, what?
—The button
that turns off the lights.[6]

Transformations of the Child and the Moon

Dunya Mikhail

FIRST IMAGE
The child raised his head to see
the moon concealed
behind the building.
Their shadows chased each other.
The building didn't know
who jumped first
to paint a red puddle
under the child's feet.

SECOND IMAGE
The child went to the river,
and as a likeness to a mirror,
the child sank
into the river's drowning moon.

THIRD IMAGE
The child raced on the beach
chasing the falling ball of the sky,
while the sand counted
the footprints of the moon
carrying the child to heaven.[7]

Seven Laments for the War-Dead

Yehuda Amichai

1

Mr. Beringer, whose son
fell at the Canal that strangers dug
so ships could cross the desert,
crosses my path at Jaffa Gate.

He has grown very thin, has lost
the weight of his son.
That's why he floats so lightly in the alleys
and gets caught in my heart like little twigs
that drift away.

2

As a child he would mash his potatoes
to a golden mush.
And then you die.

A living child must be cleaned
when he comes home from playing.
But for a dead man
earth and sand are clear water, in which
his body goes on being bathed and purified
forever. . . .

Is all of this sorrow? I guess so.
"May ye find consolation in the building
of the homeland." But how long
can you go on building the homeland
and not fall behind in the terrible
three-sided race
between consolation and building and death?[8]. . . .

Palestinian

Eli Alon

He returned to the deserted hill
thirty years after the destruction
of his village: "Here was the well . . .
here they came to draw water . . . here
the house, the grapevine, the fig tree . . ."
And I am thinking of Ein Shemer
where I was born and grew up and where
my children were born. I imagine
my son returning in thirty years
a refugee, an exile, murmuring: "Here
the dining hall . . . hand in hand with Father
on the sidewalk . . . and here the big
lawn where we used to play until
it got dark . . . Where has it all gone?
Where have they all gone to?"[9]

Not unlike children, vulnerable also is earth itself, for a long time at the mercy of human rampage. Jeremiah lamented:

How long will the land mourn,
and the grass of every field wither?
For the wickedness of those who live in it
the animals and the birds are swept away. . . . (Jer 12:4)

God lamented:

Many shepherds have destroyed my vineyard,
they have trampled down my portion,
they have made my pleasant portion
a desolate wilderness.
They have made it a desolation;
desolate, it mourns to me.
The whole land is made desolate,
but no one lays it to heart. (Jer 12:10-11)

Second, across cultures and religions, and throughout history, increasing numbers of people express sadness at our failures to live together as one human family, without conflict and devastation. Abraham Lincoln said of the U.S. Civil War:

> In great contests each party claims to act in accordance with the will of God. Both may be, and one must be, wrong. God cannot be for and against the same thing at the same time. In the present civil war it is quite possible that God's purpose is something different from the purpose of either party. . . .[10]

And a few years later, from his Second Inaugural Address:

> Both read the same Bible, and pray to the same God; and each invokes His aid against the other.[11]

Amal al-Jubouri of Iraq laments:

Veil of Religions
Amal al-Jubouri

If you are One
and your teachings are One
why did you inscribe our infancy in the Torah
and adorn our youth in the Gospels
only to erase all that in your final Book?
Why did you draw those of us who acknowledge your oneness
    into disagreement?
Why did you multiply in us, when you are the one and only One?[12]

The following prayer was composed by the Fourteenth Dalai Lama of Tibet (September 29, 1960):

Words of Truth
His Holiness Tenzin Gyatso

Humble sentient beings, tormented
by sufferings without cease,
Completely suppressed by seemingly endless

and terribly intense, negative deeds,
May all their fears from unbearable war, famine,
and disease be pacified,
To freely breathe an ocean of happiness and well-being.
And particularly the pious people
of the Land of Snows who, through various means,
Are mercilessly destroyed by barbaric hordes
on the side of darkness,
Kindly let the power of your compassion arise,
To quickly stem the flow of blood and tears. . . .

May this heartfelt wish of total freedom for all Tibet,
Which has been awaited for a long time,
be spontaneously fulfilled;
Please grant soon the good fortune to enjoy
The happy celebration of spiritual with temporal rule.[13]

Each of the three Abrahamic traditions—and all religions, really—has within it a higher ground, a beautiful vision to move beyond the base human instincts of harm, toward a unity of humankind pursuing shared values. For example:

In the Hebrew Bible

[God] shall judge between the nations,
and shall arbitrate for many peoples;
they shall beat their swords into plowshares,
and their spears into pruning hooks;
nation shall not lift up sword against nation,
neither shall they learn war anymore. (Isa 2:4)

In the New Testament

You have heard that it was said,
"You shall love your neighbor and hate your enemy."
But I say to you, love your enemies and pray for those who
       persecute you,
so that you may be children of your Father in heaven . . .
For if you love those who love you, what reward do you have?

. . . Be perfect, therefore, as your heavenly Father is perfect.
(Matt 5:43-48)

In the Qur'an

In the Torah we prescribed for them a life for a life,
an eye for an eye, a nose for a nose, a tooth for a tooth, an equal
wound for a wound:
if anyone forgoes this out of charity, it will serve as atonement
for his bad deeds. Those who do not judge according to what
God has revealed are doing grave wrong." (Sura 5:45; *Abdel
Haleem*)[14]

In each of these sacred texts, the higher ground to which humans
are called comes from God, with all human beings on an equal,
respected footing, yet secondary to God's will and greater vision. In
such a vision, the faithful are challenged to rise to the ever-higher
levels of living already inherent in their traditions, revealed by God.
It is to lament and pray (and ask for blessing upon) not just one's
own community or one's own religion or nation, but for all humanity to whom God longs to show love and compassion, and to reach
out with justice and hope. This calls for *innovation* and for *expansion*
of the traditional genre of lament. While naming and calling for the
redress of injustice, and affirming the healthy expression of anger
about hurt and injustice, a revised lament form in our time really
should *critique and correct* the misguided and horrific forms of redress
of revenge and violence. The world longs for the revealing of lament
made new, in its many cultural forms, which will lead us to a new
quality of life together in the human family, as the "children of God,"
that we might offer unqualified praise for God, who is for us all.

Proposal for a Renaissance and People's Movement

It is the people in a grassroots movement who can lead the way in
cultivating a constructive dynamic of oral traditional composition
and performance of lament for the world today. At the outset of
this book, I emphasized not only the importance of lament (as do

others) as an idea to be talked about, read in sacred texts, included in theology, preached about, not overlooked in prayer liturgy, and even as a critical component in popular music. More important than all these, in my view, is *the process of composing and performing laments*, and not just by religious or music leaders, but by all the people.

I suggest that we link the above problem of violence, and the need to innovate within the genre, with a solution inherent in the very lament traditions we have been considering. That is, traditional composition and performance of lament (and other genres) world-wide always involved not simply passing down the same songs, but innovating and transforming songs and genres to meet the sociopolitical and religious challenges of the times. The power has always been in the familiar made new, meeting immediate needs.

Cultures around the world that still practice traditional forms of singing, whether in Asia, Africa, or the Americas, often exhibit a genuinely vibrant culture, and practice of faith that is linked to a living oral traditional, popular process. There is something vital to be learned from these practices that integrate the balance of lament and praise typical in the Judaic traditions of the psalms and the biblical liberation narratives, affirmed in the Christian New Testament and the Muslim Qur'an. And yet, their beautiful religious and cultural distinctions should not be glossed over.

Without a return to what traditional cultures implicitly knew and still know—that this process is the lifeblood of a living community as it responds to the needs of its members and the social challenges around it, not just one day a week, but all the time—then especially we in the West will not mend much of the brokenness of our cultures. There is strength in those communities worldwide that have retained a traditional compositional process, regardless of what their particular religious tradition might be. Without the recognition and ongoing cultivation of such a process, which does require a matrix of community within which it can happen, then we will not revitalize, healthy communities. We will continue to allow destructive or complacent ideologies to run the world without challenge, without the people's empowerment. We will not invigorate the beloved traditions with a fresh infusion of energy and ideas. Above all, for the faithful, we will not allow God's Spirit to have a say in what we do, but will remain satisfied with a "static quo." Rather, we must recognize the importance of a process of composing lament (and praise), must cultivate the process, find avenues for it, find joy in it, affirm those who create, relinquish some control over the holding of power and over what is comfortable, find liberation while still affirming tradition, and not be threatened by change or newness. We will find that community then becomes stronger than ever, because this creative process serves the needs of the community, its culture, its religious tradition, and our callings from Beyond for the bettering of God's world.

While both scholars and political leaders have too often today avoided the link of suffering to social responsibility and policies, popular singers and poets of lament through human history have not. Thus, it is they who have often played a prophetic role—one that is sorely needed, especially for the vulnerable who have no voice over against those wielding power and violence. It is the singers and poets who must lead the world now in an innovation of lament to unite us and move us beyond violence, to challenge the politicians and the people to leave behind our old, divisive and destructive ways. Indeed, singers and poets across cultures through history have carried the popular voice, through oral traditional lyrics, shared when the reality of community was strong, as well as when disaster struck. The voices of those traditional singers and poets have been disappearing as local communities disintegrate before the bulldozer of industrial, consumerist globalization, which favors the marketing of detached, disembodied voices, or prefers prosaic media pundits, distant politicians, and military experts. However, more and more often around the globe, the voices and songs of suffering people are finding their way onto the airwaves through cyberspace, as it affords a ready and more democratic thoroughfare for urgent pleas and protest.

As noted in the sacred texts above, the seeds and winds of change are already with us—blowing across our shared human values, through our traditional customs of composing and singing, and lifting us with our higher spiritual principles. Let us join our voices for a worldwide movement for constructive change.

———————— ∞∞∞ ————————

CHAPTER EIGHT

From Tragedy to Transformation

This long journey with lament has led us to the sober realizations that children are often the greatest victims in our world, and second, that there is a worldwide sadness that we humans cannot live in peace. Yet lament leads us to still more important realizations—namely, that hopeful voices around the world have been, and already are, fashioning a tentative, daring new world.

In "Lament of a Stone," Croatian Jure Kaštelan wrote:

Return me to the rock masses, the cliffs, the mountain ranges.
Return my innocence to the laws of eternity.
. . . Rulers of the earth, give me peace and sleep.
Let not your armies clang with their hooves.
Let not the tears flow.
Tear me up from the pavement and the streets, from the thresh-
    olds of prisons and cathedrals.
Let tempests and lightning beat upon me. . . .[1]

Israeli poet Yehuda Amichai read the following poem in Oslo, Norway, for the awarding of the Nobel Peace Prize, 1994, to Yitzhak Rabin, Yasser Arafat, and Shimon Peres:

Wildpeace

Not the peace of a cease-fire,
let alone the vision of the wolf and the lamb,
but rather
as in the heart after the excitement is over,
when you can talk only about a great weariness.
I know that I know how to kill,
that's why I am an adult.
And my son plays with a toy gun that knows
how to open and close its eyes and say Mama.
A peace
without the big noise of beating swords into plowshares,
without words, without
the thud of the heavy rubber stamp: let it be
light, floating, like lazy white foam.
A little rest for the wounds—
who speaks of healing?
(And the howl of the orphans is passed from one generation
to the next, as in a relay race:
the baton never falls.)

Let it be
like wildflowers,
suddenly, because the field
must have it: a wildpeace.[2]

Anticipating the new South Africa, Mxolisi Nyezwa wrote:

Things Change

for Malope

at least then, it won't be like this
it will be a totally new suffering
like when a baby sucks his thumb.

it will be a totally new experience
(for God and history has provided)

we won't have to blow our minds
about it.

it will be like a fresh song
from a sparkling songbird
it will be like that for us, as an old
woman sits neglected
on the chair of her memories
it will be fresher, more vital
for us . . . at least it won't be like death.

and like death we die
every moment of our lives
it will be a totally new suffering
it will be like a song sung free
from a careless heart. . . .

(our failure will have its dignity.) [3]

After September 11th in New York City, Skip Shea wrote:

Songs of Mourning

I do not mourn for New York
because songs can't die
and New York is our song
America's song

yet I stand in disbelief
knowing we all die
my Shawna died
for no real reason
for no cause
and without song
just the silence of brakes

and I can't comprehend either
I can only hear the sound
of New York

emanating from Westchester Hills Cemetery
Gershwin's blues rhapsodize the
blood red of the fire stations
while from the Bronx
Miles plays his own
kind of blues to soothe us all
as Irving Berlin's
God Bless America ends with
a question mark

over in Brooklyn
Bernstein's West Side Story
has spread its borders
into Manhattan
as tragedies magnify
while Coltrane's
Love Supreme struggles
to belong

yet the sound that captures me
and my posture
is the final chord struck
by Johnny Thunders
from Flushing
reverberating
like the sound of God crying
as his creation spirals downward
once again

and I still don't mourn for New York
I will sing
because they have given me
the gift
of a song to mourn with.[4]

A journey with lament brings us to a fourth realization—that it has often been children and youth who have led the movements in the world for change, peaceful change.

A choir of five hundred schoolchildren was the first to perform "Lift Ev'ry Voice and Sing," the African-American "national anthem," for a celebration of Abraham Lincoln's birthday in 1900.

Lift Ev'ry Voice and Sing

James Weldon Johnson

Lift ev'ry voice and sing,
'Til earth and heaven ring,
Ring with the harmonies of Liberty;
Let our rejoicing rise
High as the list'ning skies,
Let it resound loud as the rolling sea.
Sing a song full of the faith that the dark past has taught us,
Sing a song full of the hope that the present has brought us;
Facing the rising sun of our new day begun,
Let us march on 'til victory is won.

Stony the road we trod,
Bitter the chastening rod,
Felt in the days when hope unborn had died;
Yet with a steady beat,
Have not our weary feet
Come to the place for which our fathers sighed?
We have come over a way that with tears has been watered,
We have come, treading our path through the blood of the
    slaughtered,
Out from the gloomy past,
'Til now we stand at last
Where the white gleam of our bright star is cast.

God of our weary years,
God of our silent tears,
Thou who has brought us thus far on the way;
Thou who has by Thy might
Led us into the light,
Keep us forever in the path, we pray.

Lest our feet stray from the places, our God, where we met Thee,
Lest, our hearts drunk with the wine of the world, we forget Thee;
Shadowed beneath Thy hand,
May we forever stand,
True to our God,
True to our native land.[5]

Tragedy struck the children of Soweto, South Africa, in their peaceful protest of school conditions, when Hector Pieterson was killed by the apartheid riot squad on June 16, 1976. The riot squad was acting against unarmed youth. But the youth of Cape Town took to the streets the next day, continuing the march. Oliver Lawrence, then twenty years old, wrote this song there:

Downtown Blues

Oliver Lawrence

When the kids started marching
There was a lesson to be learned
When the kids started marching
Pages of history would be turned

When the riot squad rolled up
They were mad at the children who
Asked for their freedom
When they should have been in school

Then the bombs started flying
Filling up all the skies
And the people started crying
When the teargas hit their eyes

Then the kids started shouting
You may have your baton and your gun
But if you try to catch us
We'll show you how we can run

When the kids started marching
Singing their freedom songs

You said it wouldn't happen
But they brought it on real strong

When the kids marched into Cape Town
There was a lesson to be learned
When the kids marched into Cape Town. . . .[6]

Children appear now to have become adopted by Mother Earth (so many are orphans) because of their long-shared suffering. Children find salve in Nature, as Rabindranath Tagore's poem "On the Seashore" suggests, where waves "like a mother" do not turn them away or discriminate, but sing to them . . .

On the Seashore
Rabindranath Tagore

On the seashore of endless worlds children meet.
The infinite sky is motionless overhead and the restless water is
    boisterous. On the seashore of endless worlds the children
    meet with shouts and dances.
They build their houses with sand, and they play with empty
    shells. With withered leaves they weave their boats and smil-
    ingly float them on the vast deep. Children have their play
    on the seashore of worlds.
They know not how to swim, they know not how to cast nets.
    Pearl-fishers dive for pearls, merchants sail in their ships,
    while children gather pebbles and scatter them again. They
    seek not for hidden treasures, they know not how to cast nets.
The sea surges up with laughter, and pale gleams the smile of
    the sea-beach. Death-dealing waves sing meaningless ballads
    to the children, even like a mother while rocking her baby's
    cradle. The sea plays with children, and pale gleams the
    smile of the sea-beach.
On the seashore of endless worlds children meet. Tempest roams
    in the pathless sky, ships are wrecked in the trackless water,
    death is abroad and children play. On the seashore of endless
    worlds is the great meeting of children.[7]

American Muslim poet Daniel Abdal-Hayy Moore wrote a beautiful tribute to all the children of the world who have died in conflict or hardship:

All the Dead Children

Daniel Abdal-Hayy Moore

Angels are learning new tricks to entertain all the
dead children
just bringing them to a quiet place used to be enough
blue panels sonorous as cool winds rising to
infinite heights and
luminous rivers tasting of fresh milk and
passionflower honey

But now they are more restless and want something
lively such as fabulous displays and real
stellar extravaganzas to shut out the memories

All the wingéd horses have been brought in
and every banner from every battle ever waged
transformed into aurora borealis brightness is
planted on either side of the great arena which is
actually nowhere you can put your finger on and may be as
big as a sparkle or light years across

The angels begin conventionally enough and since they're
anti-gravitational they are capable of some
pretty amazing feats their specialty being a
spinning array of a few billion shimmering their wings and
turning slowly at first in a
cone that goes up through so many dimensions the
children have to stop counting with
each dimension demarcated by another
color no one on earth's spectrum has
ever seen before

Then the cone begins
turning faster and faster and shoots higher and higher

finally sweeping their astonished souls wide-eyed into a
vortex so swift they barely notice that they're
arcing across fields of unearthly green and seas of
unoceanic turquoise

Each shroud has been made into a tent filled with
fabulous fruits and unidentifiable edibles of
uttermost succulence

Each soul has been given the ultimate glimpse
and the accurate portrayal
the perfect sustenance and the infinite intensity

Each time they clap their hands a new
universe appears
more fabulous than the last

And when they tire of such delights
William Blake reads to them from his new work
and Mozart comes in and plays them a tune
on a million pianos.[8]

And a response to this call . . .

They jam to instruments and drums of every land,
    thrill to Michael Jackson's moondance, then
    stilled by Luciano's high Cs, they collapse!

In the United States, youth had marched in the civil rights movement, singing "This little light of mine, I'm gonna let it shine . . . ,"[9]
and "All we are sayin' is give peace a chance" (John Lennon). More
recently, Bon Jovi and Pavarotti had sung together "Let It Rain" on
behalf of the children suffering from war around the world:[10]

. . . Children are like planting seeds,
you've got to let their flowers grow . . .
Fà che piova, (Let it rain)
Fà che il cielo mi lavi il dolor
(Let heaven wash away my pain). . . .

All these lyrics of lament move from tragedy to transformation. In South Africa, not only youth, but people of many faiths, as well as the nonreligious and the political organizers, had followed a high calling, risking their lives to overturn apartheid in a mostly nonviolent revolution. On Nelson Mandela's ninetieth birthday recently, Vusi Mahlasela led a massive crowd in singing an emotionally poignant "When You Come Back." The song (a dirge, really) remembered the tragic murder of the beloved and gifted composer of freedom songs, poet, and activist Vuyisile Mini, who was the subject of the video "Amandla!" and whose songs had inspired the movement.[11] The crowd, black and white, sang a tribute in unison, further transforming lament to liberation:

> This is the unknown grave
> The one who died maintaining his mind
> his will had been so strong and musically inclined
> his sad melody is coming out like smoke from the wood fire,
>   confessing,
> who died last night
> who died this morning
> and why
> one dangerous mind
> and four million graves
> look down into that grave
> and do not weep
> skeleton confessing
> the loss of music
> and culture and beliefs
> skeleton confessing
> the age of lamentations
> and the age of broken minds and souls
> I picked up the soil
> from this unknown grave
> and blew it up with the wind
> as to make reference one day
> and I say
> Mayibuye iAfrica.

Sing now, Africa
Sing loud and sing to the people.
Let them give something to the world and not just take from it

[Chorus] We'll ring the bells when you come back
We'll ring the bells when you come back (x4)

Our lost African music will turn into the music of the people.
Yes people's music by the people's culture and I will be the one
    who will climb up the mountain
reaching for the top of our African days while women working
    for the lazy lot, sing!

[Chorus] Africa sing, Africa sing
Africa sing, Africa sing (x8)
Sing sing Africa, sing Africa. . . .[12]

From the deepest pain, suffering, and lament, the peoples of the world amazingly are finding and are expressing a vision of great hope—for an end to violence, for healing, peace, and unity. Palestinian and Israeli youth have joined to work for peace in the movement "OneVoice."[13] Jordi Savall has united international musicians in the book/art/CD collection of music from the three Abrahamic faiths, "Jerusalem: City of the Two Peaces."[14] In Chicago, youth of different faiths and cultures have united behind leader Eboo Patel in a blossoming international movement, the Interfaith Youth Core. In Sarajevo, the Pontanima ("Spiritual Bridge") intercultural, interfaith choir has since war in the 1990s been singing one another's songs with a single voice that restores their vision of that city's former beautiful balance and blend of diversity. Is this not a vision for the world? To hear one another's laments and to join voices across cultures in compassion and justice toward healing and peace?

Perhaps it is fitting to end this book by pointing the reader to the "Playing for Change" movement now circling the world,[15] in which musicians from all over the world are united via the Internet and media technology to all sing the same song, in their beautiful diversity of sounds and images and beats and rhythms from their cultures and peoples. They have sung "Stand By Me"[16] and "One

Love" (Marley). It was the prophet Jeremiah who spoke for God to the women and mothers of long ago: *"Teach to your daughters a dirge, and each to her neighbor a lament."*

One day, perhaps, the human family will listen and learn one another's songs, and the vision and the sound will powerfully soar and resound, when the singers of the world's countries will not always have to sing the songs of America or the West. Instead, they will teach their songs, ancient and new, of lament and joy, and the peoples of the world will join in the extraordinary rhythms and words and truly sing together, finding a love for "a new song" and for each other.

Acknowledgments

Daniel Abdal-Hayy Moore, "All the Dead Children, " from *Psalms for the Brokenhearted*, published online at www.danielmoorepoetry. com/mns/psalms.html. Reprinted by permission of the author.

Eli Alon, "Palestinian," transl. Barbara Goldberg in *After the First Rain: Israeli Poems on War and Peace*, ed. Barbara Goldberg and Moshe Dor (Syracuse, N.Y.: Syracuse University Press, 1998). Reprinted by permission of Barbara Goldberg.

Lami'ah Abbas Amarah, "Tears on a Sad Iraqi Face," transl. Salih J. Altoma, *Al Jadid* 3, no. 21 (1997). Reprinted by permission of the translator and Elie Chalala, editor of *Al Jadid*.

Yehuda Amichai, "Seven Laments for the War-Dead" and "Wild-peace," transl. Chana Bloch in *The Selected Poetry of Yehuda Amichai*, ed. Chana Bloch and Stephen Mitchell (Berkeley and Los Angeles: University of California Press, 1996). Reprinted by permission of the University of California Press.

Anonymous, "Crying Over Child: To the Child Killed by Nine Gun Shots," translated by Archie C. C. Lee in *Global Bible Commentary*, ed. Daniel Patte (Nashville: Abingdon, 2004). Reprinted by permission of the translator.

Anonymous, "Lament poem #12," transl. Mishael Caspi, in *Weavers of the Songs: the Oral Poetry of Arab Women in Israel and the West Bank*, ed. Mishael Caspi and Julia Ann Blessing (Washington, D.C.: Three Continents, 1991). Reprinted by permission of the translator.

Anonymous, "Song for Sudan," reprinted under a Creative Commons license. See http://creativecommons.org/licenses/by-nc-nd/2.0/.

Borislav Arapović, "croatian psalm 137" and "Telefax from Croatia," from Borislav Arapović, *Between Despair and Lamentation*, ed. Nancy C. Lee (Elmhurst, Ill.: Elmhurst College, 2002). Reprinted by permission of the author.

"Auschwitz." Romani lament song reprinted courtesy of the U.S. Holocaust Memorial Museum.

Isaac bar Shalom, "There is No One Like You Among the Dumb," transl. William Morrow, in "The Revival of Lament in Medieval *Piyyutîm*," *Lamentations in Ancient and Contemporary Cultural Contexts*, ed. Nancy C. Lee and Carleen Mandolfo (Atlanta: Society of Biblical Literature, 2008). Reprinted by permission of the translator.

Vonani Bila, "A Visit to Oom Brown" by Vonani Bila, from *Magicstan Fires* (Elim: Timbila Poetry Project, 2006). Reprinted by permission of the author.

Black Elk, "Earth Prayer," from *Earth Prayers from Around the World*, ed. Elizabeth Roberts (New York: HarperCollins, 1991). Reprinted by permission of HarperCollins.

Brother Dash (Dasham K. Brookins), "Headline Islam," from c.d. *Poetically Speaking* (B000RY7GZG; Meem Music, 2007); text at http://brotherdash.com/?p=29. Reprinted by permission of the author.

The Dalai Lama, "Words of Truth," from www.dalailama.com. Copyright © the Office of His Holiness the Dalai Lama. Reprinted by permission of the Office of His Holiness the Dalai Lama.

Mahmoud Darwish, "I Belong There" from *Unfortunately, It was Paradise: Selected Poems* (Berkeley and Los Angeles: University of California Press, 2003). Reprinted by permission of the University of California Press.

Thomas A. Dorsey, "Take My Hand, Precious Lord," words and music copyright © 1938 by Thomas A. Dorsey, renewed by Warner-Tamerlane Publishing Corp. Reprinted by permission of Alfred Publishing Co. Inc.

Enheduanna, "Lament to the Spirit of War," translation copyright © 2009 by Daniela Gioseffi; published in Daniela Gioseffi, *Women on War: International Writings from Antiquity to the Present* (New York: Feminist Press, 2003). Reprinted by permission of the translator.

Clyde Fant, "A Lament for New Orleans," reprinted by permission of the author.

Mordecai Gebirtig, "Our Town is Burning." Reprinted courtesy of the U.S. Holocaust Memorial Museum.

Ruth Faulkner Grubbs, "Black Oak (a place)," published in the anthology *Outscape*, ed. Jessie Janeshek and Jesse Graves (Knoxville: Knoxville Writers Guild, 2008), and "Mommie," published in the collection *Holy Ground: Where Love Goes* (Knoxville: Tennessee Publishing, 2009). Reprinted by permission of the author.

Suheir Hammad, "What I Will," from *ZaatarDiva* (New York: Cypher Books, 2006). Reprinted by permission of Suheir Hammad and Cypher Books.

'Alī ibn al-Ḥusayn, "Supplication 13," transl. William C. Chittick, from *The Psalms of Islam* (Muhammadi Trust of the United Kingdom, 1988). Reprinted by permission of the translator.

Emmanuel Jal, "Gua," performed with Abdel Gadir Salim, from the CD *Ceasefire*. Reprinted by permission of Emmanuel Jal.

Amal al-Jubouri, "Veil of Religions," © 1999 by Amal Al-Jubouri and Dar Al-Saqi, London & Beirut. Reprinted by permission of the author.

Jure Kaštelan, "Lament of a Stone," transl. Ante Kadić in "Postwar Croatian Lyric Poetry," *American Slavic and East European Review* 17, no. 4 (December 1958): 523, 528. Reprinted as Fair Use from *Slavic Review.*

al Khansa' (Tumadir bint 'Amr). "Allah Watered Earth That Came to Hold Them with Morning Cloud's Downpour," transl. Arthur Wormhoudt. Reprinted by permission of Pearl Shinn Wormhoudt.

A. M. Klein, "Elegy," from *A.M. Klein: Complete Poems*, Part 2, ed. by Zailig Pollock (Toronto: University of Toronto Press, 1990). Reprinted by permission of the publisher.

Marija Koprivnjak, "Mostar, the Vukovar of Herzegovina" and "Jeremianic Lamentations over Bosnia and Herzegovina." Reprinted by permission of the author.

Mazisi Kunene, "They Are Also Children of the Earth," transl. Vusi Mchunu, *Igudu likaSomcabeko* (Van Schaik, 1997). Reprinted by permission of Mathabo Kunene.

The Lamentation over the Destruction of Sumer and Ur, transl. Piotr Michalowski. Reprinted by permission of the translator.

Oliver S. Lawrence, "Downtown Blues." Reprinted by permission of the author.

Vusi Mahlasela, "When You Come Back," on the CD *The Voice*. Reprinted by permission of the author.

Mzi Mahola, "What Will They Eat?" from *When Rains Come* (South Africa: Carapace Poets, an imprint of Snailpress, 2000), copyright © Mzi Mahola. Reprinted by permission of the author.

Dunya Mikhail, "The Artist Child" and "Transformations of the Child and the Moon," transl. Elizabeth Winslow, from *The War Works Hard* (New York: New Directions, 2005). Reprinted by permission of New Directions Publishing.

Charlie Miller, "A Prayer for New Orleans." Reprinted by permission of the author.

Neesha Mirchandani, "Meena Lives Within Us," © Neesha Mirchandani, from http://www.rawa.org/neesha2.htm. Reprinted by permission of the author.

Kadya Molodovsky, "God of Mercy," transl. by Irving Howe, from *The Penguin Book of Modern Yiddish Verse*, ed. by Irving Howe, Ruth R. Wisse and Khone Shmeruk (New York: Viking Penguin, 1987). Reprinted by permission of Viking Penguin, a division of Penguin Group (USA) Inc.

Mxolisi Nyezwa, "Things Change," from *Song Trials* (Scottsville, South Africa: University of KwaZulu-Natal Press, 2000). Reprinted by permission of the author.

Suzanne Nyiranyamibwa, "Lament of Victims of Genocide," from Faustin Kagame and Thierry Mesas, *Rwanda nziza*, with photographs by Gilles Tordjeman (Paris and Kigali: Urukundo Sepia, 2005). Reprinted by permission of http://www.orwelltoday.com/rwandapoemgenocide.shtml.

Ljubica Ostojić, "Record of the City in Blank Verse," transl. Zulejha Riđanović, *Sahat Kula* (Sarajevo: Međunarodni centar za mir, 1995). Reprinted by permission of the author.

LYRICS OF LAMENT

Quotations from Abdullah Yusuf Ali's translation of the Qur'an are from the Online Quran Project (http://al-quran.info). Reprinted by permission of the Online Quran Project.

"Rabab (Lament for Husayn)," from Lynda Clarke, "Elegy (*Marthiya*) on Husayn: Arabic and Persian," *Al-Serat* 12 (1986). Reprinted by permission of the translator.

Rachel, "To My Country," from *Flowers of Perhaps: Selected Poems of Rachel*, translated by Robert Friend (London: Menard, 1994). copyright © 1994 Jean Shapiro Cantu. Reprinted by permission of Jean Shapiro Cantu.

Moayed al-Rawi, "The Illusion of Place," transl. Noel Abdulahad, *Al Jadid* 10, no. 49 (2004). Reprinted by permission of the author and Elie Chalala, editor of *Al Jadid*.

Mustafa Khalid al-Sayfi, "Trip in the Ruins of Al-Walaja [*Rihla fi Atlal al-Walaja*]," from Abu Khiyara, 'Aziz, et al., *Al-Walaja: Hadara wa Tarikh* [Al-Walaja: Culture and History] (Amman, Jordan: Al-Walaja Cooperative Society, 1993). English translation from Rochelle Davis, "Mapping the Past, Re-creating the Homeland: Memories of Village Places in pre-1948 Palestine," in *Nakba: Palestine, 1948, and the Claims of Memory*, ed. Ahmad H. Sa'di and Lila Abu-Lughod (New York: Columbia University Press, 2007). Reprinted by permission of Rochelle Davis.

"Senzeni Na," traditional South African song, excerpt from Alton B. Pollard, III, "Rhythms of Resistance," in *This is How We Flow: Rhythm in Black Cultures* (Columbia, S.C.: University of South Carolina Press, 1999). Reprinted by permission of Alton B. Pollard, III.

Skip Shea, "Songs of Mourning," copyright © 2002 Skip Shea. Reprinted by permission of the author.

Siamanto, "The Dance," transl. Peter Balakian, *Against Forgetting* and *Bloody News from My Friend: Poems* (New York: W. W. Norton, 1993). Reprinted by permission of the translator.

Abdulah Sidran, "Planet Sarajevo," reprinted by permission of the author.

Kisan Sosa, "The inheritance," transl. G. K. Vankar, from the online journal *Muse India*, edition editor, Meena Kandasamy. Reprinted by permission of the author.

Bruce Springsteen, "My City of Ruins," copyright © 2001 Bruce Springsteen (ASCAP). Reprinted by permission. International copyright secured. All rights reserved.

Aung San Suu Kyi, "In The Quiet Land." Reprint permission recommended by the Democratic Voice of Burma on behalf of Aung San Suu Kyi, who is imprisoned.

Isaac Welch, Jr., "Children on the Trail," from *Feeding the Ancient Fires: A Collection of Writings by North Carolina American Indians* (Greensboro, N.C.: Cross Roads Press, 1999). Reprinted by permission of the North Carolina Humanities Council.

Joseph Wulf, "Sunbeams," transl. by Bret Werb. Reprinted courtesy of the U.S. Holocaust Memorial Museum.

Yu Xin, "The Lament for the South," transl. Archie C. C. Lee in his article, "Engaging Lamentations and the Lament for the South: A Cross-Textual Reading." Reprinted by permission of the translator.

Ittamar Yaoz-Kest, "Blackout," transl. Cicely Angleton and Moshe Dor, *After the First Rain: Israeli Poems on War and Peace* (New York: Syracuse University Press with Dryad Press, 1998). Reprinted by permission of Cicely Angleton.

Notes

Introduction

1. "Song for Sudan" (anonymous), performed by the international ensemble of Moussa Traore, Balla Tounkara, Dave Mattacks, Richard Thompson, Mikael Merska, Laura Cortese, and Adrian Aquirre *(Fishweasel Music, ASCAP, 2004)*.

2. A Dalit poem from the collection by Gujarati poet Kisan Sosa, posted on the online journal *Muse India*, http://www.museindia.com/show-feature.asp?id=494 accessed May 27, 2009), where Issues 9 and 11 (2006/07) included Tamil and Gujarati Dalit poems. The editor, Meena Kandasamy, suggests that "in Marathi, the word Dalit means ground crushed, broken down and reduced to pieces."

3. "Back Water Blues," performed after Hurricane Katrina by Irma Thomas from the CD, *Our New Orleans: A Benefit Album for the Gulf Coast* (B000BNTM0U; Nonesuch Records, 2005); listen to Irma Thomas's performance of the song on the NPR Web site, http://www.npr.org/templates/story/story.php?storyId=5703300 (accessed February 28, 2009); or an excerpt at http://www.nonesuch.com/albums/our-new-orleans (see especially the work of the "17 Poets" of New Orleans, featured on PBS television (http://pbs-newshour.onstreammedia.com/cgi-bin/visearch?user=pbs-newshour&template=play220asf.html&query=%2A&squery=%2BClipID%3A6+%2BVideoAsset%3Apbsnh041006&inputField=%20&ccstart=3015632&ccend=3335319&videoID=pbsnh041006) led by Dave Brinks and Megan Burns (accessed April 10, 2006).

4. A. M. Klein, "Elegy," in *Truth and Lamentation: Stories and Poems on the Holocaust*, ed. Milton Teichman and Sharon Leder (Urbana: University

of Illinois Press, 1994) 435–40 (orig. publ. *A.M. Klein: Complete Poems*, ed. Zailig Pollock, University of Toronto Press, 1990).

5. Moayed al-Rawi, "The Illusion of Place," trans. Noel Abdulahad, in *Al Jadid*, 10, no. 49 (Fall 2004), and in the online journal *Al Jadid: A Review and Record of Arab Culture and Arts*, 8, no. 38 (Winter 2002), http://leb.net/~aljadid/poetry/TheIllusionofPlace.html (accessed June 9, 2009).

6. Black Elk, "Earth Prayer," online: http://www.firstpeople.us/FP-Html-Wisdom/BlackElk.html (accessed September 21, 2009); first line: "Hey, Lean to Hear My Feeble Voice," in Elizabeth Roberts, *Earth Prayers* (New York: HarperCollins, 1991), 86. Reprinted by permission of Harper-Collins Publishers.

7. Interview with Elie Wiesel by Timothy K. Beal, in *Strange Fire: Reading the Bible after the Holocaust*, ed. Tod Linafelt (New York: New York University Press, 2000), 23.

8. Brian Wren, *Praying Twice: The Music and Words of Congregational Song* (Westminster John Knox, 2000), esp. 290–5; see also Wren's reference to other composers of lament themes today, including Ruth Duck and Shirley Murray, and a review of others' work by Paul Westermeyer in *Let Justice Sing: Hymnody and Justice* (American Essays in Liturgy; Collegeville, Minn.: Liturgical Press, 1998). See Miriam Therese Winter's 1993 lyrics for "America the Beautiful," at http://www.breadblog.org/2007/10/daily-justice-1.html (accessed August 11, 2009).

9. Wilma Bailey, "The Lament Traditions of Enslaved African American Women and the Lament Traditions of the Hebrew Bible," in *Lamentations in Ancient and Contemporary Cultural Contexts*, ed. Nancy C. Lee and Carleen Mandolfo (Atlanta: SBL, 2008), 51–162.

10. "Prayer for New Orleans," music and lyrics by Charlie Miller, from the CD *Our New Orleans*; to view Miller's performance of the song, go to his Web site, http://www.charliemiller.us/prayer_no/prayer_no.html; (accessed May 27, 2009).

Chapter 1

1. Poem by Nancy C. Lee, January 19, 2009.

2. Piotr Michalowski, trans., *The Lamentation over the Destruction of Sumer and Ur* (Winona Lake, Ind.: Eisenbrauns, 1989), 39–62. Italics designate a doubtful translation of a known text, or indicate transliteration; square brackets have been employed for restorations in the text; round brackets have been put around interpolations made for a better understanding of the translation.

3. Samuel Kramer, "Lamentation over the Destruction of Ur," in *Ancient Near Eastern Texts Relating to the Old Testament, with Supplement*, 3rd

ed., ed. J. B. Pritchard (Chicago: Princeton University Press, 1969), 611–19.

4. Translation adapted and edited Daniela Gioseffi, ed., *Women on War: International Writings from Antiquity to the Present* (New York: Feminist Press at City University of New York, 2003), 3.

5. Suheir Hammad,"What I Will," performance online: http://www.youtube.com/watch?v=LFbE8RBhSDw (accessed June 8, 2009), cited on the book companion Web site; [interview online: http://leb.net/~aljadid/interviews/DropsofSuheirHammad.html] (accessed September 21, 2009).

6. See Gail Holst-Warhaft, "Mourning in a Man's World: the *Epitaphios Logos* and the Banning of Laments in Fifth-Century Athens," *Dangerous Voices: Women's Laments and Greek Literature* (London: Routledge, 1992); in early Christianity, women's laments for the dead may have continued in individual cultures in spite of church opposition, but in liturgy, women's lament was given expression in commemorating Mary's lament for her son Jesus and women singing the Psalms in the church (Holst-Warhaft, 4, 6).

7. In *Diwan al Khansa*, trans. from the text of Karim Bustani by Arthur Wormhoudt (Arab translation series, 1 [5]; Oskaloosa, Iowa: William Penn College, 1973), 101–2, at "Other Women's Voices: Translations of Women's Writing before 1700," http://home.infionline.net/~ddisse/khansa.html (accessed September 8, 2008).

8. Translation by Omar S. Pound, in Elizabeth Warnock Fernea and Basima Qattan Bezirgan, eds., *Middle Eastern Muslim Women Speak: Al-nisā almuslima almuslimat fi alSharq alusat yathadathn Zanān-i musulmani Khāvār-i mianih su Khan miguyand* (Austin: University of Texas Press, 1977), 5.

9. Joseph Suad and Afsaneh Najmabadi, eds., *Encyclopedia of Women & Islamic Cultures* (Leiden: Brill, 2003), 118–22; Leor Halevi, *Muhammad's Grave* (New York: Columbia University Press, 2007), 114–142.

10. "A Short History of Women in Black," http://www.womeninblack.org/eryhistory.html (accessed December 16, 2008).

11. Anonymous author, trans. Archie C. C. Lee, from *Dagong Bao*, a Hong Kong newspaper, June 18, 1989, quoted by Lee in "Lamentations," in Daniel Patte, et al., eds., *Global Bible Commentary* (Nashville: Abingdon Press, 2004), 229.

12. Neesha Mirchandani, "Meena Lives within Us," http://www.rawa.org/neesha2.htm (accessed January 5, 2009). Other poems and songs for listening can also be found on the RAWA Web site.

13. Jean Calmard, "Ḥosayn B. ʿAli," http://www.iranica.com/newsite/index.isc?Article=http://www.iranica.com/newsite/articles/v12f5/v12f5036c.

html (accessed January 2, 2009); Muhammad-Reza Fakhr-Rohani, "The Maqtal Genre: A Preliminary Inquiry and Typology," http://www.imamreza.net/eng/imamreza.php?id=7165 (accessed January 2, 2009); Annemarie Schimmel, "Karbala and the Imam Ḥusayn in Persian and Indo-Muslim literature," *Al-Serat* 12 (1986), http://www.al-islam.org/al-serat/Karbala-Schimmel.htm (accessed August 1, 2009).

14. Lynda Clarke, "Elegy (*Marthiya*) on Ḥusayn: Arabic and Persian," *Al-Serat* 12 (1986), http://www.al-islam.org/al-serat/default.asp (accessed January 10, 2009).

15. In Persian and Urdu, the term is *marsiya*.

16. Clarke, "Elegy (*Marthiya*) on Ḥusayn."

17. See Ḥosayn-Wāʿeẓ Kāšefi (d. 910/1504–1505) and his *Rawżat al-šohadāʾ*, which synthesized eulogy and elegy materials that became important for Twelver Shiʾism, and Moḥtašam Kāšāniʾs (d. 996/1587 or 1000/1591) *Davāzdah band* that became a model for further elegies, homilies, and dirges for Moḥarram ceremonies, cited in Calmard, "Ḥosayn B. ʿAli"; see also Schimmel, "Karbala and the Imam Ḥusayn," Fakhr-Rohani, "The Maqtal Genre."

18. Though extreme self-injury was condemned by the Shiʾite ulama (legal scholars); Jean Calmard, "Ḥosayn B. ʾAli"; Jewish tradition expresses an aversion to the ritual cutting of oneself practiced by other cultures/religions; thus with regard to the Baal worshippers, see 1 Kgs 18:26-28.

19. Ibid.

20. Clarke, "Elegy (*Marthiya*) on Ḥusayn."

21. Islam From Inside, "Mourning Ḥusayn (On Matam)," http://www.islam-frominside.com/Pages/Articles/Mourning%20Husayn%20(Matam%20for%20Husayn).html (accessed January 2, 2009).

22. Brother Dash, "Headline Islam," http://brotherdash.com/?p=29 (accessed August 23, 2009). You can listen to Brother Dash's spoken poetry on the Web site.

23. Walt Whitman, "O Captain, My Captain," *Selected Poems* (New York: Random House Value Publishing, 1992), 211.

24. "When lilacs last in the door-yard bloom'd: A Requiem 'For those we love'" / Als Flieder jüngst mir im Garten blüht: Ein Requiem "Für die, die wir lieben" (1946), English text by Walt Whitman, music and German text by Paul Hindemith. C. Ed. 7, 2, http://www.rhapsody.com/-search?query=when%20lilacs%20last&searchtype=RhapAlbum (accessed June 10, 2009); for more information on Hindemith, see http://www.hindemith.org/E/summary.htm (accessed June 10, 2009).

25. Listen to the song at http://www.ushmm.org/museum/exhibit/online/music/detail.php?content=zunem_shtrain (accessed June 10, 2009).

26. Composer and author of lyrics unknown; listen to a performance by the group Khanci Dos at http://www.ushmm.org/museum/exhibit/online/music/detail.php?content=khanci (accessed June 10, 2009).

27. "Abraham, Martin, and John," written by Dick Holler (B000MMLMR6; Ace Records UK, 2007; orig. recorded 1968); lyrics at http://www.lyricsmode.com/lyrics/d/dion/abraham_martin_and_john.html (accessed August 1, 2009); to listen to the instrumental tune, go to http://www.rhapsody.com/karaoke-dion (accessed June 10, 2009).

28. Bob Dylan composed a song in tribute and lament for the deaths of King, Gandhi, and Jesus, called "They Killed Him," found on the album, *Knocked Out Loaded* (1986); listen to an excerpt at http://www.bobdylan.com (accessed June 10, 2009).

29. "Candle in the Wind 1997," music by Elton John, lyrics by Bernie Taupin.

30. From the CD *Songs from the Westcoast* (B000VWOD82; Universal Records, 2001); to listen to an excerpt, go to http://www.amazon.com/American-Triangle/dp/B000VWOD82/ref=sr_1_1?ie=UTF8&s=dmusic&qid=1245072554&sr=8-1 (accessed June 15, 2009).

Chapter 2

1. Mishael M. Caspi and Julia Ann Blessing, *Weavers of the Songs: The Oral Poetry of Arab Women in Israel and the West Bank* (Washington, D.C.: Three Continents, 1991), 103; originally published by M. Caspi in "'My Brother, Vein of My Heart': Arab Laments for the Dead in Israel," *Folklore* 98 (1987), 28–40.

2. *The Songs Are Free: Bernice Johnson Reagon and African-American Music*, videocassette, produced and directed by Gail Pellett (Films for the Humanities and Sciences 6774; Arlington, Va.: Public Broadcasting Service, c. 2005).

3. Carleen Mandolfo, *God in the Dock: Dialogic Tension in the Psalms of Lament* (JSOTS 356; Sheffield: Sheffield Academic, 2002).

4. A. Z. Idelsohn, *Jewish Music in its Historical Development* (1929; repr., New York: Schocken Books, 1967).

5. Hedwig Jahnow, *Das hebräische Leichenlied im Rahmen der Völkerdichtung* (The Hebrew Funeral Song in the Context of Folk Poetry) (BZAW 36; Giessen: Alfred Töpelmann, 1923), 98–101, 171, 178.

6. Translation of "slain Bat-'Ammi ['daughter of my people']" by the author; many commentators understand this to be a metaphor or personification that refers to the city of Jerusalem and its people. I have argued that it could also refer to a real individual woman whom Jeremiah refers to as Bat-'Ammî, who was a casualty in the siege.

7. Jure Kaštelan, trans. Ante Kadić, in "Postwar Croatian Lyric Poetry," *American Slavic and East European Review* 17, no. 4 (1958): 523.

8. Poet anonymous, poem #12, in Mishael M. Caspi and Julia A. Blessing, *Weavers of the Songs: The Oral Poetry of Arab Women in Israel and the West Bank* (Boulder, Colo.: Lynne Rienner, 1991), 125–26.

9. Jacob Glatstein, "Nightsong," trans. Ruth Whitman, in *Truth and Lamentation: Stories and Poems on the Holocaust*, ed. Milton Teichman and Sharon Leder (Urbana: University of Illinois Press, 1994), 473.

10. Abdulah Sidran, "Planet Sarajevo," trans. D. Dostal, in *Blind Man Sings to His City* (Sarajevo: Međunarodni centar za mir, 1997), 11–17.

11. Marija Koprivnjak, "Mostar, the Vukovar of Herzegovina," in *Ratni Blagoslovi* (Osijek: Izvori, 1996), 138–39, first publ. in 1992; English translation, first three lines of selection by J. Berković and R. Pađen, last two lines by Nancy C. Lee.

12. Archie Chi Chung Lee, "Engaging Lamentations and the Lament for the South: A Cross-Textual Reading," in *Lamentations in Ancient and Contemporary Cultural Contexts*, ed. Nancy C. Lee and Carleen Mandolfo (Atlanta: Symposium 43; SBL, 2008), 125–38.

13. John Hollow Horn, in James Wilson, *The Earth Shall Weep: A History of Native America* (New York: Grove Press, 1998), xi; the poem is also available at http://www.republicoflakotah.com/?page_id=668 (accessed January 26, 2009).

14. New American Standard Bible translation.

15. Ibid.

16. Verses 1a and 5 from the NRSV; verses 1b, 2, and 4 translated by the author.

17. A. M. Klein, "Elegy," in Teichman and Leder, *Truth and Lamentation*, 435–40.

18. Mustafa Khalil al-Sayfi, "Trip in the Ruins of Al-Walaja [Rihla fi Atlal al-Walaja],"cited in Rochelle A. Davis, "Mapping the Past, Re-creating the Homeland: Memories of Village Places in pre-1948 Palestine," in *Nakba: Palestine, 1948, and the Claims of Memory*, ed. Ahmad H. Sa'di and Lila Abu-Lughod (New York: Columbia University Press, 2007), 65–66; from Abu Khiyara, 'Aziz, et al. *Al-Walaja:Hadara wa Tarikh* [Al-Walaja: Culture and History] (Amman, Jordan: Al-Walaja Cooperative Society, 1993), 76.

19. Davis, "Mapping the Past, Re-creating the Homeland," 66–67.

20. Slavica Crnjac, "Vukovar," trans. Dalia Kuća, in *Pismo iz rasapa* [Writing from Turmoil], ed. Đurđa Miklauzić (Zagreb: Multimedijski ženski centar NONA, 1995), 16.

21. From Ljubica Ostojić, "Record of the City in Blank Verse," trans. Zulejha Riđanović, in *Sahat kula* (Sarajevo: Međunarodni centar za mir, 1995), 77–92.

22. Suzanne Nyiranyamibwa, "Lament of Victims of Genocide," http://www.orwelltoday.com/rwandapoemgenocide.shtml (accessed January 12, 2009); published in the book by Faustin Kagame and Thierry Mesas, with photographs by Gilles Tordjeman, *Rwanda nziza* (Paris and Kigali: Urukundo Sepia, 2005).

23. Claus Westermann, *Praise and Lament in the Psalms* (Louisville: Westminster John Knox, 1981), 52–81, 165–213.

24. John (Fire) Lame Deer and Richard Erdoes, from "Looking at the Sun, They Dance," in *Lame Deer, Seeker of Visions* (New York: Pocket Books, 1994), 208–24.

25. Ibid.

26. http://www.zangomusic.com/lasuandsa.html.

27. U2, War (Island Records, B000O2TTS8-CD, 1983) http://u2.com/discography/lyrics/lyric/song/127 (accessed September 14, 2009); for a study of the significant lament poetry tradition in Ireland (caoineadh and keening), see Angela Bourke, "More in Anger than in Sorrow: Irish Women's Lament Poetry: The Irish Traditional Lament and the Grieving Process," Women's Studies International Forum 11, no. 4 (1988), 287–91.

28. Jean Paul Samputu, *Testimony from Rwanda* (MCM4003-CD; Stephen McArthur, Multicultural Media, 2004), also available at http://worldmusic.nationalgeographic.com/worldmusic/view/page.basic/artist/content.artist/samputu_21026 (accessed June 7, 2009).

29. To listen to the song performed by Harmonius Serade Choir, go to http://www.last.fm/music/Harmonius%2BSerade%2BChoir%2B%252 6%2BVusi%2BMahlesela (accessed June 7, 2009); lyrics quoted from A. B. Pollard's study, "Rhythms of Resistance," in *This Is How We Flow: Rhythm in Black Cultures*, ed. Angela M. Nelson (Columbia, S.C.: University of South Carolina Press, 1999), 98–124.

30. Borislav Arapović, *Between Despair and Lamentation*, ed. Nancy C. Lee; trans. I. Pozajić Jerić; (Elmhurst, Ill.: Elmhurst College, 2002); see also his collections in Croatian: *Iz noćnog dnevnika* (From the Night Diary, 1989), *Tamnionik* (Darkhouse, 1992), and *Kamenopis* (Stonescript, 1993).

Chapter 3

1. *The Tanakh*, Stone Edition (Brooklyn: Mesorah Publications, 1998), 8.

2. However, in the Jewish aggadot, Cain faces his death with the seventh generation that follows him; his great-grandson Lamech accidentally shoots him in a hunting accident. See *The Legends of the Jews*, trans. Henrietta Szold (Philadephia: Jewish Publication Society, 1937), 1:115–17.

3. Louis Ginzberg, *The Legends of the Jews* (6 vols. + index; Philadelphia: Jewish Publication Society, 1968), 1:110. Ginzberg compiled these and

many other stories, and the rabbinic teachings on them (dated from the second to the fourteenth centuries), in his classic multivolume work. The complete set is now available online through Project Gutenberg: http://www.gutenberg.org/etext/1493 (accessed June 11, 2009).

4. *The Qur'an*, trans. M. A. S. Abdel Haleem (Oxford: Oxford University Press, 2005), 70.

5. Ricardo J. Quinones, *The Changes of Cain: Violence and the Lost Brother in Cain and Abel Literature* (Princeton: Princeton University Press, 1991).

6. Ginzberg, *Legends of the Jews*, 1:65.

7. Ibid., 70, 79.

8. Ibid., 80.

9. Ibid., 80–89, 91–102.

10. A historical range of interpretations from the Abrahamic faiths of the Garden of Eden story can be found in Mishael M. Caspi, with Mohammad Jiyad, *Eve in Three Traditions and Literatures: Judaism, Christianity, and Islam* (Lewiston, N.Y.: Edwin Mellen, 2004), and Kristen E. Kvam, Linda S. Schearing, and Valarie H. Ziegler, eds., *Eve & Adam: Jewish, Christian, and Muslim Readings on Genesis and Gender* (Bloomington: Indiana University Press, 1999).

11. There are about twenty references to the exodus in the New Testament and in the Qur'an.

12. Walter Brueggemann, *The Prophetic Imagination* (Philadelphia: Fortress Press, 1978), 15–27.

13. Ibid., 20–22.

14. For example, see the early work of James H. Cone (African American), *A Black Theology of Liberation* (New York: Lippincott, 1970); Gustavo Gutiérrez (Peruvian), *Teologia de la Liberacion: Perspectivas* (Salamanca: Ediciones Sígueme, 1972) [*A Theology of Liberation* (Maryknoll: Orbis, 1973)]; Choan Seng Song (Taiwanese), *Third-Eye Theology: Theology in Formation in Asian Settings* (Guildford and Lowden: Lutterworth Press, 1979); Archbishop Desmond Tutu (South African), "We Drink Water to Fill Our Stomachs," in *The Rainbow People of God* (New York: Doubleday, 1994), 25–40, "The Story of Exodus" (essays 1 & 2), in *Hope and Suffering* (Johannesburg: Skotaville Publishers, 1983), 49–60; *The Cambridge Companion to Liberation Theology*, ed. Christopher Rowland (New York: Cambridge University Press, 2007); R. S. Sugirtharajah, ed., *Voices from the Margin* (Maryknoll: Orbis, 1995), 215–85, and the interpretations of exodus there from Latin American, Korean, black African, Asian, Palestinian, and Native American perspectives.

15. See especially the work of Musa W. Dube (Botswana), *Postcolonial Feminist Interpretation of the Bible* (St. Louis, Mo.: Chalice, 2000).

16. For a study of the narrative and a recent context of genocide, as well as consideration of the problematic of the deity taking the life of the Pharaoh's son as retributive punishment, see Nancy C. Lee, "Genocide's Lament: Moses, Pharaoh's Daughter, and the Former Yugoslavia," in *God in the Fray: Essays in Honor of Walter Brueggemann*, ed. Tod Linafelt and Timothy K. Beal (Minneapolis: Fortress Press, 1998).

17. On terminology, see Patrick Miller's study, *They Cried to the Lord* (Minneapolis: Fortress Press, 1994), 38–48; see also Samuel E. Balentine, *Prayer in the Hebrew Bible: The Drama of Divine-Human Dialogue* (Overtures to Biblical Theology; Minneapolis: Fortress Press, 1993).

18. Ibid.

19. Ibid.

20. For a study of the story's helpful critique of genocide, and a critique of the glossing over by commentators of how God is portrayed, see Lee, "Genocide's Lament."

21. For example, in Rabbi Nathan Goldberg's translation of and commentary to *The Passover Haggadah* (Jersey City, N.J.: KTAV, 1987): "It is customary to spill a drop of wine for each of the ten plagues and catastrophes that struck the Egyptians. The reason for this is that although the Egyptians oppressed our people cruelly, our cup of joy cannot be complete because the freeing of the Israelites entailed suffering for the enemy. Rabbi Judah (in the following paragraph) could not bring himself even to mention the plagues, and so he devised an abbreviation consisting of their initial letters . . . The Rabbinic tradition on the Red Sea episode is singularly unvindictive. God Himself is seen as reproaching the angels for singing hymns of glory upon the miraculous overthrow of the Egyptians: 'The works of My hands are drowning in the sea, and you offer songs of praise!' Accordingly, during the last days of Passover, commemorating the miracle at the Red Sea, the synagogue liturgy calls for a recitation of half-*Hallel* (part of the Hymns of Praise) rather than the complete service" (16n5 and 17n6).

22. James Cone, *The Spirituals and the Blues: An Interpretation* (New York: Seabury, 1972), 1, 7.

23. Melva Wilson Costen, *African American Christian Worship*, 2nd ed. (Nashville: Abingdon, 2007), 33.

24. Listen to an excerpt of "Go Down, Moses," sung by Paul Robeson, and find more information on "The Spirituals Project" at http://ctl.du.edu/spirituals/Performing/robeson.cfm (accessed June 5, 2009); for a full performance, go to http://www.youtube.com/watch?v=gtLcELU1brA (accessed June 5, 2009); lyrics from http://www.negrospirituals.com/news-song/go_down_moses2.htm (accessed June 4, 2009).

25. Wilda Gafney, *Daughters of Miriam: Women Prophets in Ancient Israel* (Minneapolis: Fortress Press, 2008), 76–85.

26. Some biblical interpretations that would be sympathetic to recent feminist and womanist interpretations go as far back as the earliest understandings of the tradition and text; more recent feminist and womanist interpreters of Miriam, usually considered within liberationist perspectives, include the early work of Phyllis Bird, "Images of Women in the Old Testament," in *Religion and Sexism: Images of Women in the Jewish and Christian Traditions*, ed. Rosemary R. Reuther (New York: Simon & Schuster, 1974); Elizabeth Schüssler Fiorenza, "Interpreting Patriarchal Traditions," in *The Liberating Word: A Guide to Nonsexist Interpretation of the Bible*, ed. Letty Russell (Philadelphia: Westminster, 1976); and most recently, Wilda Gafney.

27. Phyllis Trible, *Texts of Terror: Literary-Feminist Readings of Biblical Narratives* (Overtures to Biblical Theology; Minneapolis: Fortress Press, 1984). See also Denise Ackermann, "Tamar's Cry: Re-reading an Ancient Text in the Midst of an HIV/AIDS Pandemic," in *Character Ethics and the Old Testament*, ed. M. D. Carroll and J. E. Lapsley (Louisville: Westminster John Knox, 2007), 191–219; Ackermann, "The Language of Lament," *The Other Side* 39, no. 4 (2003): 26–29.

28. See especially Naomi Graetz for her studies on women's silence and perspectives in biblical stories, for example, *S/He Created Them: Feminist Retellings of Biblical Tales* (Gorgias Press LLC, 2003), and *Unlocking the Garden: A Feminist Jewish Look at the Bible, Midrash, and God* (Gorgias Press LLC, 2004).

29. Renita Weems, *Battered Love: Marriage, Sex, and Violence in the Hebrew Prophets* (Overtures to Biblical Theology; Minneapolis: Fortress Press, 1995); Carleen Mandolfo, *Daughter Zion Talks Back to the Prophets: A Dialogic Theology of the Book of Lamentations* (Atlanta: SBL, 2007); Christl M. Maier, *Daughter Zion, Mother Zion: Gender, Space, and the Sacred in Ancient Israel* (Minneapolis: Fortress Press, 2008); Julia M. O'Brien, *Challenging Prophetic Metaphor: Theology and Ideology in the Prophets* (Louisville: Westminster John Knox, 2008).

Chapter 4

1. Mayer I. Gruber, *Rashi's Commentary on Psalms* (Philadelphia: Jewish Publication Society, 2007); William Morrow, *Protest against God: The Eclipse of a Biblical Tradition* (Sheffield, England: Phoenix, 2007); Mitchell Dahood, *Psalms* (3 vols.; Anchor Bible; Garden City: Doubleday, 1966–1970); Walter Brueggemann, *The Message of the Psalms* (Augsburg Old Testament Studies; Minneapolis: Augsburg, 1984), *Praying the Psalms* (Winona, Minn.: Saint Mary's Press, 1986), and *Israel's Praise: Doxology Against Idolatry and Ideology* (Minneapolis: Fortress Press, 1988); Samuel E. Balentine, *Prayer in the Hebrew Bible*; James

Luther Mays, *Psalms* (Interpretation; Louisville: Westminster John Knox, 1994); Patrick D. Miller, *They Cried to the Lord*; William P. Brown, *Seeing the Psalms: A Theology of Metaphor* (Louisville: Westminster John Knox, 2002); Carleen Mandolfo, *God in the Dock: Dialogic Tension in the Psalms of Lament* (JSOTS 356; Sheffield, 2002).

2. For a study of this theme in biblical lament, see Samuel E. Balentine, *The Hidden God: The Hiding of the Face of God in the Old Testament.* (New York: Oxford University Press, 1983).

3. See especially Robert P. Gordon, ed., "A Story of Two Paradigm Shifts," in *The Place is Too Small for Us: The Israelite Prophets in Recent Scholarship* (SBTS; Winona Lake, Ind.: Eisenbrauns, 1995), 9.

4. Mandolfo, *God in the Dock.*

5. William P. Brown's study, *Seeing the Psalms*, explores the Psalms' metaphors of refuge, pathway, trees, sun and light, water, animals, the "anatomy" of a personal God, and divine roles.

6. An interesting insight comes from African American musicologist, Bernice Johnson Reagon, who suggests that the early "I" songs of the spirituals and black churches were also sung for and by the voice of the whole community; "I" also meant "all of us." She suggests the "I" was changed to "we" for inclusiveness, when people from outside the community joined the civil rights movement, for example, "We Shall Overcome" (*The Songs Are Free: Bernice Johnson Reagon and African-American Music,* videocassette, produced and directed by Gail Pellett (Films for the Humanities and Sciences 6774; Arlington, Va.: Public Broadcasting Service, c. 2005).

7. NRSV followed unless otherwise stated.

8. See, for example, David R. Blumenthal, *Facing the Abusing God.*

9. Recent commentaries and studies include Scott A. Ellington, "Risking the World in Job," *Risking Truth: Reshaping the World through Prayers of Lament* (Eugene, Ore.: Pickwick, 2008), 94–129; Samuel E. Balentine, *Job* (Smyth & Helwys Bible Commentary; Macon, Ga.: Smyth & Helwys, 2006); Carol Newsom, *The Book of Job: A Contest of Moral Imaginations* (New York: Oxford University Press, 2003); Leo G. Perdue and W. Clark Gilpin, eds., *The Voice from the Whirlwind: Interpreting the Book of Job* (Nashville: Abingdon, 1992); David J. A. Clines, *Job*, 2 vols. (WBC; Dallas: Word Books, 1989); Gustavo Gutiérrez, *On Job: God-Talk and the Suffering of the Innocent* (Maryknoll: Orbis, 1987); J. Gerald Janzen, *Job* (IBC; Atlanta: John Knox, 1985).

10. An intertextual parallel could be explored between Job and Cain; for both, God protects their life from being taken. Yet Cain is guilty of wrong; Job claims he has done no wrong to deserve punishment. His friends essentially claim that surely Job is reaping what he has sown.

11. Job 1–2.

12. Cf. Sophia Richman, "Finding One's Voice: Transforming Trauma into Autobiographical Narrative," *Contemporary Psychoanalysis* 42 no. 4 (2006): 639–50.

13. King James Version.

14. Verse 19 translated by author.

15. See Gerald O. West, "The Poetry of Job as a Resource for the Articulation of Embodied Lament in the Context of HIV and AIDS in South Africa," in Lee and Mandolfo, *Lamentations in Ancient and Contemporary Cultural Contexts*; and West with Bongi Zengele, "Reading Job 'Positively' in the Context of HIV/AIDS in South Africa," *Concilium* 4 (2004): 112–24. See also Ken Stone, "Safer Text: Reading Biblical Laments in the Age of AIDS," *Theology & Sexuality* 10 (1999): 16–27. The place of funeral services or rituals in the handling and explanation of deaths caused by AIDS is of great importance in changing the traditional stigma about AIDS; see Thomas Cannell, "Funerals and AIDS, Resilience and Decline in KwaZulu-Natal," *Journal of Theology for Southern Africa* 125 (2006): 21–37.

16. *God on Trial*, DVD.

17. Kadya Molodovsky, "God of Mercy," in Teichman and Leder, eds., *Truth and Lamentation*, 427.

18. A. M. Klein, "Elegy," in Teichman and Leder, eds., *Truth and Lamentation*, 435–40.

19. To read the lyrics, go to http://www.bobdylan.com/#/songs/death-emmett-till (accessed June 10, 2009).

20. "Blowin' in the Wind" by Bob Dylan (copyright 1962; renewed 1990 Special Rider Music); http://www.bobdylan.com/#/songs/blowin-wind (accessed June 9, 2009), to listen to an excerpt there.

21. There are far fewer studies on lament in the New Testament, and they are contained within larger works; see William Holladay, *The Psalms through Three Thousand Years: Prayerbook of a Cloud of Witnesses* (Minneapolis: Fortress Press, 1993); Balentine, *Prayer in the Hebrew Bible*; Miller, *They Cried to the Lord*; Ellington, *Risking Truth*.

22. Mary F. Foskett, "Luke" in *The Discipleship Study Bible* (Louisville: Westminster John Knox, 2008), 1785. In *Rachel's Cry: Prayer of Lament and Rebirth of Hope*, Kathleen D. Billman and Daniel L. Migliore suggest that Mary's praise is "steeped in prophetic faith" (Cleveland: United Church Press, 1999), 3.

23. Foskett, "Luke," *Discipleship Study Bible*.

24. See Gail R. O'Day, "Surprised By Faith: Jesus and the Canaanite Woman," *Listening* 24 (1989): 290-301.

25. NRSV; a shorter version is in Luke 11:2–4.

26. Holladay, *Psalms through Three Thousand Years*, 115–133.

27. Ibid.
28. The NIV translation seems to miss the shift in verb tense at this critical moment.
29. Scott Ellington, *Risking Truth*, 168.
30. Cf. John Ehle, *Trail of Tears: The Rise and Fall of the Cherokee Nation* (New York: Doubleday, 1988), 345–46, 392; *Cherokee Perspective: Written by Eastern Cherokees*, ed. Laurence French and Jim Hornbuckle (Boone, N.C.: Appalachian Consortium Press, 1981), 24–25.
31. Listen to a traditional Cherokee lament song, "On the trail where they cried", performed by Eddie Bushyhead on the CD "The Blue Clan Ani Sa Kho Ni Project" (Cherokee, Wild Cherry Productions, 1988); can be ordered through the link n.p. [June 14 2009]; Online: http://www.cherokeemuseum.org/Merchant2/merchant.mvc?Screen=PROD&Store_Code=CM&Product_Code=05832&Category_Code=M.
32. In *Feeding the Ancient Fires: A Collection of Writings by North Carolina American Indians*, ed. MariJo Moore (Greensboro, N.C.: Cross Roads Press, 1999), 73.
33. Called "sorrow songs" by W.E.B. Du Bois; n.p. [cited 2 August 2009]; Online: http://ctl.du.edu/spirituals/Survival/sorrow.cfm. See Wilma Bailey, "The Lament Traditions of Enslaved African American Women and the Lament Traditions of the Hebrew Bible," in *Lamentations in Ancient and Contemporary Cultural Contexts*, ed. Nancy C. Lee and Carleen Mandolfo, 151–62.
34. James Cone, *Spirituals and the Blues*, 108–42.
35. Arthur C. Jones, "Paul Robeson," in *The Spirituals Project (2004)*, http://ctl.du.edu/spirituals/Performing/robeson.cfm (accessed June 5, 2009), from Paul Robeson's autobiography, *Here I stand* (1958; repr., Boston: Beacon Press, 1971).
36. This would be a different understanding than some biblical commentators' tendency to suggest that the psalmist promised to praise God in order primarily to motivate God to act. The spirituals and blues tradition suggests that the singing in anticipation of something better actually evoked it, by freely tapping into the sacred, larger realm.
37. Quoted from *Jazz*. DVD, dir. Ken Burns (Arlington, Va: Public Broadcasting Service, 2001).
38. Ibid.
39. Ibid.
40. Listen to the song "Couldn't Hear Nobody Pray," sung by Sam McClain, from the film *Jubilee Singers*, at http://www.pbs.org/wgbh/amex/singers/sfeature/songs.html (accessed June 4, 2009).
41. Arthur C. Jones, "The Choral Tradition" on the Web site "Sweet Chariot: the Story of the Spirituals," http://ctl.du.edu/spirituals/Performing/

choral.cfm (accessed June 9, 2009); Reagon quote from a partial transcript of Reagon's Veterans of Hope Project interview, reprinted in *Sojourners Magazine*, August, 2004.

42. *Bill Moyers Journal*, Bernice Johnson Reagon interview; http://www.pbs. org/moyers/journal/11232007/watch3.html (accessed June 9, 2009); see also Bernice Johnson Reagon and African American Music, *The Songs Are Free*.

43. Costen, *African American Christian Worship*, 90.

44. Victor Parachin, "Story Behind the Song: Thomas A. Dorsey's 'Precious Lord, Take My Hand'"; http://www.christianitytoday.com/tc/2003/julaug/16.16.html?start=2 (accessed June 9, 2009).

45. Mahalia Jackson performance, n.p. (accessed August 2, 2009), http://www.dailymotion.com/video/x4ydis_mahalia-jackson-take-my-hand-precio_music.

46. Lyrics quoted from http://cyberhymnal.org/htm/p/l/pltmhand.htm (accessed June 9, 2009); words and Music by Thomas A. Dorsey © 1938 (Renewed), Warner-Tamerlane Publishing Corp.

47. For example, "Respiration" by Mos Def, Talib Kweli, and Common, from the CD *Blackstar*, featuring Common; (B000067CLT; Rawkus Records, 2002); http://www.youtube.com/watch?v=WiNwTL0HQRI&feature=player_embedded (accessed June 10, 2009).

48. Video of Common's performance, produced by Will.i.am for the film, *Freedom Writers*; http://www.youtube.com/watch?v=XBa55sDTIiA (accessed June 10, 2009); lyrics quoted from http://www.metrolyrics.com/i-have-a-dream-lyrics-common.html (accessed June 10, 2009).

49. View a performance online at http://www.dailymotion.com/video/x1ouou_lauryn-hill-ziggy-marley_music.

50. See the Beatles Lyrics Archive: http://www.beatleslyricsarchive.com/viewSong.php?songID=185 (accessed June 9, 2009).

51. "Holy Mother" by Eric Clapton and Stephen Bishop, from the CD by Eric Clapton and Luciano Pavarotti, *Pavarotti and Friends for War Child* (452900-2DH; Digital Sound, 1996); online http://www.youtube.com/watch?v=2ziHZoCnyfs&feature=related (accessed June 9, 2009).

52. Translated by Vusi Mchunu, lyrics quoted from http://southafrica.poetryinternationalweb.org/piw_cms/cms/cms_module/index.php?obj_id=11280 (accessed June 10, 2009); from *Igudu likaSomcabeko* (Van Schaik, 1997).

53. Mzi Mahola, in *When Rains Come* (South Africa: Carapace Poets, an imprint of Snailpress, 2000), copyright Mzi Mahola; see http://southafrica.poetryinternationalweb.org/piw_cms/cms/cms_module/index.php?obj_id=5480 (accessed June 10, 2009).

54. Ibid., 192–7.

55. Ibid.

56. A *kombi* is a VW-type bus.
57. From *Magicstan Fires* (Elim: Timbila Poetry Project, 2006) copyright Vonani Bila; http://southafrica.poetryinternationalweb.org/piw_cms/cms/cms_module/index.php?obj_id=12615 (accessed June 10, 2009).
58. Ruth Faulkner Grubbs, *Holy Ground: Where Love Goes* (Knoxville: Tennessee Publishing, 2009).
59. Ibid.
60. "Allah," of course, is the Arabic term for "God," cognate to "Elohim" in Hebrew. Jews, Christians, and Muslims worship the same God.
61. "Introduction," in Imam Zayn Al-'Abidīn 'Alī ibn al-Ḥusayn, *The Psalms of Islam*, trans. William C. Chittick (London: Muhammed Trust, 1988), xxii–xxxv.
62. See Mahmoud M. Ayoub, *The Qur'an and Its Interpreters* (Albany: SUNY, 1984).
63. "Peace Be Upon Him"; this is the regularly stated phrase of reverence for Muhammad by Muslims whenever they refer to him.
64. *The Holy Qur'an*, trans. Abdullah Yusuf Ali (Ware, Hertfordshire: Wordsworth Editions, 2001). Different translations of the Qur'an can be found on the Web site http://al-quran.info (accessed June 10, 2009).
65. Michael Anthony Sells, *Approaching the Qur'an: The Early Revelations* (Ashland, Ore.: White Cloud Press, 2007); Sells's book includes a companion audio CD with numerous reciters of the Qur'an from Shi'a and Sunni traditions, and in different styles. To listen to several different recitations of the Opening (*al-Fatiha*) of the Qur'an, go to http://www.jannah.org/quran/ (accessed June 10, 2009); to listen also with English translation, scroll down further to the MP3 recording.
66. There are additional texts that allude more briefly to prayer, including 2:3, 40-46, 67-71, 89, 142-153, 197-202; 3:38-43; 4:43, 101-103, 106-107, 142-143, 148, 162; 5:6-7; 6:40-41, 52, 56, 71-72, 92; 14:31; 16:51-55; 21:73; 26: 217-220; 28:21, 88; 29:30; 35:12-18, 29-30, 36-37, 40; 40:7-9, 13-17, 26, 49, 56-60, 73-74; and 96:9-10.
67. For a study of Arabian poetry, see Michael Sells, trans. and introduction, *Desert Tracings: Six Classic Arabian Odes* (Middletown, Ct.: Wesleyan Univ. Press, 1989).
68. Animals or creatures are referred to as part of Allah's world who perform their duties faithfully.
69. "25 Duas from the Holy Quran"; http://www.islam101.com/quran/Duas25Quran.htm, citing http://www.jannah.org (accessed June 1, 2009).
70. One of the only treatments of Umm Kulthum in the West is a DVD about her, *Umm Kulthum: A Voice Like Egypt*, dir. Michal Goldman (B000K0YG8M: AFD, 2007).

71. Imam Zayn Al-'Abidīn, 'Alī ibn al-Ḥusayn, *The Psalms of Islam*, trans. William C. Chittick (London: Muhammed Trust, 1988), 48–51.
72. See Mahmoud M. Ayoub, *Redemptive Suffering in Islam* (The Hague, Netherlands: Mouton Publishers, 1978).
73. See especially the classic studies by A. Z. Idelsohn, *Jewish Liturgy and Its Development* (New York: Schocken, 1967); Idelsohn, *Jewish Music in Its Historical Development* (New York: Schocken, 1967); Feuer and Gold, *The Complete* Tishah B'Av *Service*; Holladay, *The Psalms through Three Thousand Years*; Harold W. Attridge and Margot E. Fassler, *Psalms in Community: Jewish and Christian Textual, Liturgical, and Artistic Traditions* (Symposium 25; Atlanta: SBL, 2003); Brian Wren, "Telling the Truth Through Tearful Songs," *Journal for Preachers* 26, no. 2 (2003): 22–36; Karlfried Froehlich, "Discerning the Voices: Praise and Lament in the Tradition of the Christian Psalter," *Calvin Theological Journal* 36 (2001):75–90; Bert Polman, "The Role of Lament in American Musical Life: Concerto in Three Movements," *Calvin Theological Journal* 36 (2001): 91–102; Leor Halevi, *Muhammed's Grave: Death Rites and the Making of Islamic Society* (New York: Columbia University Press, 2007); Ali J. Hussain, "The Mourning History and the History of Mourning: The Evolution of the Ritual Commemoration of the Battle of Karbala," *Comparative Studies of South Asia, Africa, and the Middle East* 25, no. 1 (2005): 78–88; Annemarie Schimmel, "Karbala and Imam Ḥusayn in Persian and Indo-Muslim Literature," *Al-Serat* 12 (1986), online journal, http://www.al-islam.org/al-serat/default.asp?url=Karbala-Schimmel.htm (accessed September 16, 2009).

Chapter 5

1. These are found in Jer 11:18-23; 12:1-6; 13:15-17; 14:13, 17-18; 15:10, 15-18; 16:19-20; 17:14-18; 18:19-23; 20:7-18; the people's laments are found, for example, in Jer 14:7-9, 19-22.
2. Nancy C. Lee, *The Singers of Lamentations: Cities under Siege, from Ur to Jerusalem to Sarajevo* (Leiden: E. J. Brill, 2002); see also, Lee, "The Singers of Lamentations: (As)scribing (De)Claiming Poets and Prophets," in Lee and Mandolfo, *Lamentations in Ancient and Contemporary Cultural Contexts*, 33–46.
3. For a full analysis, see Lee, *Singers of Lamentations*, 47–162.
4. Author's translations in this and following texts.
5. NRSV.
6. Author's translation.
7. NRSV in this text and following.
8. Nahum Sarna, Aaron Rothkoff, Joseph Braslavi, and Bathja Bayer, "Rachel," in *Encyclopaedia Judaica*, eds., Michael Berenbaum and Fred

Skolnik, vol. 17, 2nd ed. (Detroit: Macmillan Reference, 2007), 47–49; "Rachel Laments for Her Children" (*Rahel Mevakkah al Baneha*) is performed by cantors; listen to an excerpt of a contemporary arrangement by Rita Leonard at http://www.cdbaby.com/cd/rabbirita (accessed September 19, 2009).

9. Trans. Nancy C. Lee, from *Ratni Blagoslovi* (Osijek: Izvori, 1996), 135, first published in *Izvori* magazine (1992).

10. Excerpts from "Oh God, How Long Can We Go On?" in Tutu, *Rainbow People of God*, 15–21.

11. Rabindranath Tagore (his own English translation), also called by a longer title, "Jodi Tor Dak Shune Keu Na Ashe" ["If They Answer Not to Thy Call"], in *Gitanjali (Song Offerings): A Collection of Prose Translations Made by the Author from the Original Bengali* (London: MacMillan, 1913); to hear an excerpt, go to http://www.amazon.com/Ekla-Cholo-Re/dp/B00120B3EO/ref=sr_1_1?ie=UTF8&s=dmusic&qid=1244709742&sr=8-1 (accessed June 11, 2009).

12. The military dictatorship.

13. Quoted from http://dassk.org/index.php/topic,701.0.html (accessed June 10, 2009).

Chapter 6

1. David R. Blumenthal returns to lament prayer to God, written anew in light of the Shoah and other abusive situations, in *Facing the Abusing God: A Theology of Protest* (Louisville: Westminster John Knox, 1993).

2. See the dramatization, *God on Trial*, Masterpiece Theatre (DVD), written by Frank Cottrell Boyce; directed by Andy de Emmony (Arlington, Va.: Public Broadcasting Service, 2009); Marvin A. Sweeney, *Reading the Hebrew Bible after the Shoah: Engaging Holocaust Theology* (Minneapolis: Fortress Press, 2008); Dorothee Soelle, *The Silent Cry: Mysticism and Resistance*, trans. B. and M. Rumscheidt (Minneapolis: Fortress Press, 2001); Tod Linafelt, "Zion's Cause: The Presentation of Pain in the Book of Lamentations," in *Strange Fire: Reading the Bible after the Holocaust*, ed. T. Linafelt (New York: New York University Press, 2000), 267–79, and Linafelt, *Surviving Lamentations: Catastrophe, Lament, and Protest in the Afterlife of a Biblical Book* (Chicago: University of Chicago Press, 2000); Richard L. Rubenstein, "Job and Auschwitz," in *Strange Fire*, 233–51; Steven Kepnes, "Job and Post-Holocaust Theodicy," in *Strange Fire*, 252–66; Emil Fackenheim, *The Jewish Bible after the Holocaust* (Bloomington: Indiana University Press, 1991).

3. Parts of this Lamentations essay are drawn from Nancy C. Lee, "Lamentations," in *The Discipleship Study Bible*, ed. Bruce Birch et al. (Louisville: Westminster John Knox, 2008), 1116–26. Recent commentaries

and studies include Carleen Mandolfo, *Daughter Zion Talks Back to the Prophets: A Dialogic Theology of the Book of Lamentations* (Semeia Studies: Atlanta: SBL, 2007); Paul R. House, *Lamentations* (WBC; Nashville: Thomas Nelson, 2004); Kathleen O'Connor, *Lamentations and the Tears of the World* (Maryknoll: Orbis, 2002); Adele Berlin, *Lamentations: A Commentary* (Louisville: Westminster John Knox, 2002); Lee, *The Singers of Lamentations*; F.W. Dobbs-Allsopp, *Lamentations: A Bible Commentary for Teaching and Preaching* (IBC; Louisville: Westminster John Knox, 2002); Dobbs, *Weep, O Daughter of Zion: A Study of the City-Lament Genre in the Hebrew Bible* (BibOr 44; Rome: Pontifical Biblical Institute, 1993); Erhard Gerstenberger, *Psalms, Part 2, and Lamentations* (FOTL 15; Grand Rapids: Eerdmans, 2001); Linafelt, *Surviving Lamentations*; Johan Renkema, *Lamentations* (HCOT; Leuven: Peeters, 1998); Claus Westermann, *Lamentations: Issues and Interpretations* (Minneapolis: Fortress Press, 1994), and Iain Provan, *Lamentations* (NCBC; Grand Rapids: Eerdmans, 1991).

4. Cf. Jeffrey Kauffman, ed., *Loss of the Assumptive World: A Theory of Traumatic Loss* (New York: Brunner-Routledge, 2002); Judith Herman, *Trauma and Recovery: The Aftermath of Violence—from Domestic Abuse to Political Terror* (New York: Basic Books, 1997); Elaine Scarry, *The Body in Pain: The Making and Unmaking of the World* (New York: Oxford University Press, 1985).

5. Avrohom Chaim Feuer and Avie Gold, *The Complete* Tishah B'Av *Service* (New York: Mesorah, 1991).

6. Translation by the author.

7. The following is Linafelt's translation, in *Surviving Lamentations*, 59–60.

8. William S. Morrow, "The Revival of Lament in Medieval *Piyyuṭim*," in Lee and Mandolfo, *Lamentations in Ancient and Contemporary Cultural Contexts* 146–150.

9. Ibid., 146–150.

10. Peter Balakian reports that Siamanto was arrested with 250 other Armenian cultural leaders on April 24, 1915, in Constantinople by the government at the onset of the genocide and later executed along with the majority of Armenian cultural leaders; Siamanto, "The Dance," trans. Peter Balakian and Nevart Yaghlian, in Carolyn Forché, *Against Forgetting: Twentieth Century Poetry of Witness* (New York: W. W. Norton, 1993), 57–59; poem from Siamanto, *Bloody News from My Friend: Poems* (Wayne State University Press, 1996).

11. "Our Town is Burning," lyrics and music by Mordecai Gebirtig, performed on the U.S. Holocaust Memorial Museum Web site by Daniel Kempin; http://www.ushmm.org/wlc/media_so.php?lang=en&ModuleId=10005213&MediaId=2621 (accessed June 7, 2009).

12. A. L. Strauss, "Lament for the European Exile," trans. A. C. Jacobs, in *Truth and Lamentation: Stories and Poems of the Holocaust*, ed. M. Teichman and S. Leder (Urbana: University of Illinois Press, 1993), 460.

13. Emphasis added to highlight the allusion; D. Tutu, *Rainbow People of God*, 101.

14. Ljubica Ostojić, trans. Zulejha Riđanović, in *Sahat Kula* (Sarajevo: Međunarodni centar za mir, 1995), 79.

15. *Borislav Arapović:* in "Telefax from Croatia," *Between Despair and Lamentation*, ed. Nancy C. Lee, trans. I. Posajić Jerić (Elmhurst, Ill.: Elmhurst College, 2002), 28–31; "Telefaks iz Hrvatske," from the anthology *Ratni blagoslovi.*

16. The Supreme Being in the traditional spirituality of Rwanda.

17. Words and music by Suzanne Nyiranyamibwa; song quoted in the book by Gilles Tordjeman, Thierry Mesas, and Faustin Kagame, *Rwanda Nziza* (Urukundo, 2005), 87; poem quoted on the Web site http://www.orwell-today.com/rwandapoemgenocide.shtml (accessed June 11, 2009).

18. Bruce Springsteen, from *The Rising* (B000069HKH; Sony Records, 2002); lyrics and listen to excerpt at http://www.brucespringsteen.net/songs/MyCityOfRuins.html (accessed August 1, 2009); copyright Bruce Springsteen (ASCAP).

19. Clyde Fant, "A Lament for New Orleans" in N.C. Lee and C. Mandolfo, *Lamentations in Ancient and Contemporary Cultural Contexts* (SBL/Brill, 2008), 215–217.

20. Listen to an excerpt at http://www.amazon.com/Best-Ladysmith-Black-Mambazo-Wiseman/dp/B00000I2I5/ref=pd_rhf_p_t_2 (accessed June 14, 2009); from the CD *The Best of Ladysmith Black Mambazo* (B00000I2I5; Warner Bros., 2000; originally recorded with Paul Simon, 1986).

21. Rachel, "To My Country," from *Flowers of Perhaps: Selected Poems of Rachel*, trans. Robert Friend (London: Menard, 1994); http://international.poetryinternationalweb.org/piw_cms/cms/cms_module/index.php?obj_id=3271 (accessed May 25, 2009).

22. Mahmoud Darwish, "I Belong There," trans. by Carolyn Forché and Munir Akash; http://www.poets.org/viewmedia.php/prmMID/16585 (accessed May 29, 2009) from Mahmoud Darwish, *Unfortunately, It Was Paradise*, trans. and ed. Munir Akash and Carolyn Forché with Sinan Antoon and Amira El-Zein (Univ. of Calif., 2003).

23. Jamal Khambar, quoted in Kimberly Wedeven Segall, "Lamenting the Dead in Iraq and South Africa: Transitioning from Individual Trauma to Collective Mourning Performances," in Lee and Mandolfo, *Lamentations in Ancient and Contemporary Cultural Contexts*, 177–94; an earlier version appeared in *Comparative Studies of South Asia, Africa and the Middle East* 25, no. 1 (2005): 138–51.

24. Lami'ah Abbas Amarah, "Tears on a Sad Iraqi Face," trans. Salih J. Altoma, in *Al Jadid* 3, no. 21 (1997); http://leb.net/~aljadid/poetry/Tears%20 on%20a%20Sad%20Iraqi%20Face.html (accessed June 8, 2009).

25. For the most recent update of the millions affected by genocide in Sudan, and to help, go to the Web site, Save Darfur, http://www.save-darfur.org/content (accessed June 10, 2009).

26. From the CD *Ceasefire* (B000AR9ZBI; Riverboat Records, 2005); to listen to a performance of "Gua," go to http://www.youtube.com/ watch?v=53wG2Voa4PY (accessed June 7, 2009); for information on the charity that Emmanual Jal formed, Gua Africa, go to http://www. gua-africa.org/index.php (accessed June 7, 2009); an excerpt of the film about him, *War Child*, at http://www.warchildmovie.com (accessed June 7, 2009).

27. For information on the current plight of the people in the Congo, and to find out how to help, go to http://www.congowomen.org/video (accessed June 10, 2009); see also http://www.genocidewatch.org/ (accessed June 10, 2009); for the photo installation tour, go to http:// www.congowomen.org/tour/ (accessed June 10, 2009).

Chapter 7

1. René Girard's seminal work goes behind, or beyond, religion to the primary human psychological and social causes of violence; see *Violence and the Sacred*, trans. P. Gregory (Baltimore: Johns Hopkins, 1979).

2. See examples in Hedwig Jahnow's classic study, *Das hebräische Leichenlied im Rahmen der Völkerdichtung* ("The Hebrew Funeral Song in the Context of Folk Poetry") (BZAW 36; Giessen: Alfred Töpelmann, 1923); for a large perspective on war and nonviolence in the Hebrew Bible, see Susan Niditch's important work, *War in the Hebrew Bible: A Study in the Ethics of Violence* (Oxford Univ. Press, 1993).

3. A. Rashied Omar, "Conflict and Violence," *Encyclopedia of Islam and the Muslim World*, ed. Richard C. Martin (New York: Macmillan Reference USA, 2004), 1:157–160.

4. Ittamar Yaoz-Kest, "Blackout," trans. Cicely Angleton, in Moshe Dor and Barbara Goldberg, eds., *After the First Rain: Israeli Poems on War and Peace* (New York: Syracuse University Press with Dryad Press, 1998), 145.

5. Dan Pagis, "Written in Pencil in the Sealed Railway-Car," trans. Stephen Mitchell, in *Truth and Lamentation: Stories and Poems on the Holocaust*, ed. Milton Teichman and Sharon Leder (Urbana: University of Illinois Press, 1994), 491.

6. Dunya Mikhail, "The Artist Child," trans. Elizabeth Winslow, in *The War Works Hard* (New York: New Directions, 2005; orig. publ. in *Almost Music*, 1997), 54–55.

7. Dunya Mikhail, "Transformations of the Child and the Moon," in *The War Works Hard*, 71.

8. Yehuda Amichai, "Seven Laments for the War-Dead," trans. Chana Bloch, in *After the First Rain*, 7–10.

9. Eli Alon, "Palestinian," trans. Barbara Goldberg, in *After the First Rain*, 3.

10. *The Collected Works of Abraham Lincoln*, edited by Roy P. Basler, Vol. V, "Meditation on the Divine Will" (September 2, 1862?), 403–4.

11. Lincoln's Second Inaugural Address, March 4, 1865.

12. Amal al-Jubouri, "Veil of Religions," trans. Seema Atalla; http://iraq.poetryinternationalweb.org/piw_cms/cms/cms_module/index.php?obj_id=519&x=1 (accessed May 24, 2009).

13. At http://www.dalailama.com/page.21.htm (accessed June 10, 2009).

14. Trans. M.A.S. Abdel Haleem (Oxford University Press, 2005), 72.

Chapter 8

1. Jure Kaštelan, "Lament of a Stone," in Ante Kadić, "Postwar Croatian Lyric Poetry," *American Slavic and East European Review* 17 (1958): 528.

2. Yehuda Amichai, "Wildpeace," trans. Chana Bloch and Ariel Bloch, in *After the First Rain: Israeli Poems on War and Peace*, ed. Moshe Dor and Barbara Goldberg (New York: Syracuse University Press with Dryad Press, 1998), 12.

3. Mxolisi Nyezwa, "Things Change," from *Song Trials* (Scottsville, South Africa: University of KwaZulu-Natal Press, 2000); http://southafrica.poetryinternationalweb.org/piw_cms/cms/cms_module/index.php?obj_id=5474&x=1 (accessed August 11, 2009).

4. Skip Shea, "Songs of Mourning"; http://poetry.about.com/library/weekly/aa091102b.htm (accessed June 5, 2009). The power of music for many people in healing is evident; listen particularly to the performance of "Lament and Restoration" by a survivor of 9/11, at http://cdbaby.com/cd/ronwasserman1 (accessed June 15, 2009).

5. "Lift Ev'ry Voice and Sing," lyrics by James Weldon Johnson, music by John Rosamond Johnson; http://www.naacp.org/about/history/levas_history/ (accessed June 15, 2009).

6. Oliver Lawrence, "Downtown Blues," composed 1976.

7. Rabindranath Tagore, "On the Seashore"; http://rpo.library.utoronto.ca/poem/2578.html (accessed June 15, 2009); orig. publ. Rabindranath Tagore, *The Crescent Moon* (London: Macmillan, 1918), 3–4.

8. Daniel Abdal-Hayy Moore, "All the Dead Children," from *Psalms for the Brokenhearted* (published by The Ecstatic Exchange, 2006); http://www.danielmoorepoetry.com/about.html (accessed June 15, 2009).

9. Listen to the song performed by Sweet Honey in the Rock; http://www.rhapsody.com/sweet-honey-in-the-rock/freedom-song (accessed June 15, 2009).

10. Lyrics by Jon Bon Jovi, Michele Centonze, Veris Giannetti, arr. Rob Mathes, from the CD "Pavarotti & Friends for the Children of Liberia" 289460600-2; pub London: Decca Record Co. Ltd., 1998; view on n.p. [cited August 4 2009]; Online; http://www.youtube.com/watch?v=Yv APRIwX5KU&NR=1&feature=fvwp.

11. *Amandla!: A Revolution in Four Part Harmony*, prod. Desireé Markgraaff, Lee Hirsch, Sherry Simpson, Johnathan Dorfman, and Temple Fennell (B0000C2IWO; Artisan Home Entertainment, 2003, DVD).

12. Vusi Mahlasela, "When You Come Back," on the CD *The Voice* (B00009YXH1; Ato Records, 2003); http://www.youtube.com/vusimahlasela.

13. "One Voice," at http://www.onevoicemovement.org/mediacenter/mediacenter.html#MediaVideos (accessed June 15, 2009).

14. Jordi Savall and Montserrat Figueras, with Hesperion XXI, Jerusalem: *City of the Two Peaces*, book and CD (B001GAQR50; Alia Vox, 2009).

15. "Playing for Change," at http://www.youtube.com/user/PlayingForChange, and http://www.youtube.com/watch?v=Us-TVg40ExM; see musicians playing in New Orleans on http://playingforchange.com/episodes/3/One_Love (accessed June 15, 2009).

16. "Stand By Me," written by Methodist minister and gospel music composer Charles Albert Tindley in 1905.

Index of Ancient Sources

Index of Subjects